A LIFE IN FIFTY BOOKS

ANTHONY CHEETHAM

In November 1966,
by way of Mexico City, Eton College,
Balliol College, Oxford, and a Norwegian
raspberry farm, Anthony Cheetham entered the
doors of a publishing company for the first time
to begin work as a junior editor.

Fifty-eight years later he could look back
on a career in which he had shaped the landscape
of post-war British publishing to a significant
degree, having established such prominent
and notably successful companies as Century,
Orion, Quercus and Head of Zeus, and launched
imprints – from Abacus in 1973 to Zephyr in 2017
– that continue to flourish in the third decade
of the twenty-first century.

Starting with Homer's *Odyssey* and ending with
works by the evolutionary biologist Richard
Dawkins and the German historian Ernst
Kantorowicz, Anthony Cheetham has selected fifty
books as mileposts with which to map the course
of his long and productive career.

Many of these are titles that he himself published (*Dune, The Thorn Birds, A Suitable Boy, Meetings with Remarkable Trees, The Girl with the Dragon Tattoo*); some are books he wished he had published (Stephen Hawking's *A Brief History of Time*); others are simply masterworks that left an indelible mark on him (*The Lord of the Rings, War and Peace*).

A Life in Fifty Books is an affectionate and revelatory account of a publishing life remarkable for its longevity, its entrepreneurial energy and for the breadth and catholicity of its output – which runs the gamut of seriousness from academically distinguished works of history, science and philosophy to *Confessions of a Window Cleaner*.

Full of encounters with remarkable individuals as well as extraordinary books, *A Life in Fifty Books* is an engagingly written survey of an industry which, in its author's well-chosen words, offers its practitioners 'a passport to roam across the entire spectrum of human experience, endeavour and belief'.

A LIFE IN

ANTHONY
CHEETHAM

FIFTY
BOOKS

HEAD
of ZEUS

First published in the UK in 2025
by Head of Zeus Ltd,
part of Bloomsbury Publishing Plc

9 7 5 3 1 2 4 6 8

A catalogue record for this book is available from the British Library.
ISBN (HB): 9781035912766
ISBN (E): 9781035914739

Designed by Isambard Thomas at Corvo
Cover design by Jessie Price
(*The Yellow Books*, 1887 Vincent van Gogh / Bridgeman Images)
Colour separation by Dawkins Colour
Printed and bound by Elma Basim, Turkey

Bloomsbury Publishing Plc
50 Bedford Square, London, WC1B 3DP, UK
Bloomsbury Publishing Ireland Limited,
29 Earlsfort Terrace, Dublin 2, D02 AY28, Ireland

To find out more about our authors and books visit www.headofzeus.com
For product safety related questions contact productsafety@bloomsbury.com

Head of Zeus
5–8 Hardwick Street
London ECIR 4RG

WWW.HEADOFZEUS.COM

For Georgina
Genau

The Puppet Show of Memory
1943–2024

Memory can be a misleading guide to the remembrance of times past. Memory is composed of snapshots from which we try to assemble a coherent narrative. These snapshots are in turn triggered not by the events alone, but by the emotions we experience at the time: hopes and fears, joy and dismay, longings and regrets.

I have borrowed the title of my prologue from the autobiography of Maurice Baring, a former staff officer in the Royal Air Force and a prolific writer who published his memoir in 1922. I like the notion that memory is indeed a puppet show.

Here goes.

I

Vienna
1946–9

My part in the Cold War

I was born on 12 April 1943 in the French Hospital on the Avenue of the Viceroys in Mexico City. My father was a junior diplomat in the British Legation. A year later we flew to New York and joined a convoy bound for Liverpool. It was one of the largest convoys of the war, ferrying troops across the Atlantic for the D-Day invasion of Normandy.

In 1946 my father was seconded to the Allied Control Commission in Vienna. The city was a wreck, bombed out by both sides in the dying days of the war and now sliced up into four sectors by the victors. Our first apartment was on the second floor of a block overlooking an alley that marked the boundary between the Soviet and British zones.

The Cold War was about to begin. Every morning, at dawn, a column of Soviet tanks patrolled the alley, crunching the cobblestones and making a fearsome racket. Spurred on by the gleeful encouragement of my older brother, Jamie, I struck my first blow for Western democracy by emptying the contents of the broom cupboard on the lead tank. I don't suppose the tank commander even noticed.

A while later we moved into a rather grand villa in the Viennese suburb of Hietzing, where my mother commissioned a neighbouring artist to sketch my portrait. The artist complained that she couldn't do her job unless I sat still and stopped fidgeting. In order to facilitate this, she told me the whole story of Odysseus and his journey home to Ithaca from Troy, from beginning to end, over several sittings. The portrait now hangs on my bedroom wall. It shows a five-year-old boy who hangs with rapt attention on her every word.

ooooo

Some other early memories: A visit to the street market in St Stephen's Square, next to the bombed-out skeleton of the cathedral. The vendors are selling bananas, the first shipment since the war. Germans of all stripes adore bananas. The crowd is bubbling with joy. A banana is pressed into my hands. The taste is, frankly, unexciting. But I am the son of a diplomat and I can tell from the look on the faces around me that a more enthusiastic response is expected. I oblige.

Clean clothes, brushed hair, no holes in my jumper. I'm on my way to my first day at my first school, the local kindergarten. Fiercely whispered advice from my team: Do

1. *The Odyssey*

Tell me about a complicated man.
Muse, tell me how he wandered
and was lost when he had
wrecked the holy town of Troy...

The first lines in Emily Wilson's translation of *The Odyssey* (2017)

THE

ODYSSEY

HOMER

Translated by EMILY WILSON

not talk about the war. I was thoroughly confused. What war? Surely it was the Russians, not the Austrians who were our enemies?

One afternoon when I was on my way home from the kindergarten, a train with an endless number of carriages came to a halt on the level crossing at the end of our street. The carriage windows were open and packed with soldiers waving their caps in the air and yelling at the tops of their voices. I was told that they were Austrian soldiers repatriated from Soviet POW camps. The sheer joy and thunder of their relief at coming home alive has remained imprinted on my mind ever since.

My mother taught me how to read when I reached my fifth birthday. As a birthday present she gave me an enchanting book entitled *A Squirrel Called Rufus* (1941) by Richard Church. It was about a troupe of red squirrels whose woods have been invaded by their bigger and stronger grey cousins. I thought it was every bit as exciting as the adventures of Odysseus.

She read the first fifteen pages to me out loud, then told me that I would have to read the rest of the story for myself. Which I did, but only after ripping out the first fifteen pages in a temper tantrum. Seventy-five years later, the emasculated copy of Mr Church's masterwork is still in my library.

ooooo

On my last day at school, my teacher, Anna, gave me a farewell present, a book of fairy tales from the Brothers Grimm, *The Frog Prince And Other Stories*. She kissed me on both cheeks and everybody stood up to wave me goodbye.

The most important person in my life during the Vienna years was my nanny, Liesl Zabransky, who remained part of my life until her death on 20 June 1979. Liesl was a figure with a tragic past and an equally cruel future. She had spent much of the war under internment in Romania. She emerged from the camps to find that her fiancé had been killed, and made her way back to Vienna, where she took charge of my brother Jamie and myself. Post-war Vienna was an economic basket case of bombed-out buildings, food shortages and unemployment. British diplomats were under instruction to provide as many domestic jobs as possible. In our household these included Otto the chauffeur, Josef the cook and Liesl the nanny. Otto entertained us with tales of his wartime exploits on the beaches of Calais during the Battle of Britain. Josef was the bad-tempered and scary ogre who ruled the subterranean world of the kitchen and the coal cellar and threatened to lock me up in the latter with the king of the rats. Liesl took charge out of doors. We lit candles to the Virgin Mary in the magnificent cathedral churches of Vienna and visited the landmarks of the Habsburg empire.

She also introduced me to a trio of honorary aunts, who coddled me with infinite kindness and treated me to plum cake and apple strudel. I was known to them as *Der Knirps*, the whippersnapper.

When he was seven years old, my older brother was banished to an English prep school. My parents were engaged in an endless round of cocktail parties and diplomatic receptions.

I had gone native, more Austrian than English, having acquired a ripe Viennese working-class accent and a vocabulary to match. It was only years later that I realised I was fluent in Yiddish, a dialect developed by Ashkenazi Jewish emigrés who had fled persecution in Poland and Russia in earlier times.

ooooo

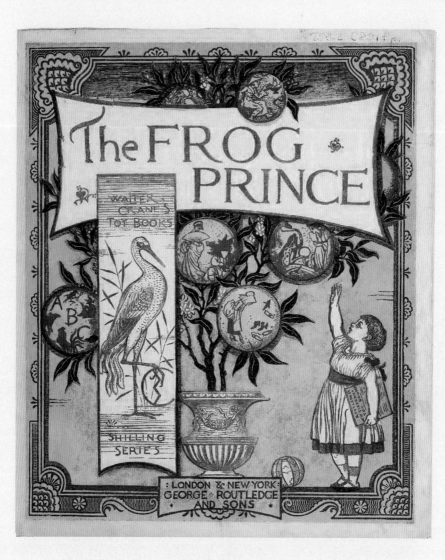

The FROG PRINCE

WALTER
CRANE'S
TOY BOOKS

A
B
C

SHILLING
SERIES

: LONDON & NEW YORK :
GEORGE ROUTLEDGE
AND SONS

All this came to an end in a car crash on the Semmering Pass en route to a skiing holiday in the Austrian Alps. As our car swerved off the road to avoid collision with an on-coming lorry, Liesl moved across the back seat to shield me from the ski sticks in the front. I was knocked unconscious. She, however, was pierced in the brain and lost the sight of an eye. Not a day went by in the rest of her life when she did not suffer from severe discomfort or acute pain. She survived in this state until her death, at the age of seventy, on 16 June 1979.

Before my father was recalled to London in 1949, I made Liesl a promise that I would one day treat her to lunch at the famous Hotel Sacher on the Ringstrasse, followed by a performance at the Vienna State Opera House. This was a promise I was able to fulfil some twenty years later. It was my very modest way of thanking her for having saved my life.

2. *The Frog Prince and Other Stories*

One fine evening a young princess put on her bonnet
and clogs, and went out to take a walk by herself in
a wood; and when she came to a cool spring of water,
that rose in the midst of it, she sat herself down
to rest a while.

The opening words of '*The Frog Prince*', translated by Edgar
Taylor and Marian Edwardes (1912)

2

Summer Fields
1950–5
Of Ringwraiths and Pederasts

Mens Sana In Corpore Sano
'A healthy mind in a healthy body'
Summer Fields school motto

At the age of seven I was enrolled at a boy's prep school
in Oxford. Summer Fields had a formidable reputation
for preparing boys to win scholarships at Eton. The teaching
was indeed exemplary, but I also remember the school as
a spartan boot camp and a refuge for paedophiles.

We were woken at 7am to stand naked in line for a
cold bath, followed by an early class, a brief service in the
chapel, a breakfast of porridge or corn flakes, and a bracing
outdoor run in the grounds.

The classroom was the domain of Geoffrey Bolton, a
dedicated classicist and ruthless disciplinarian whose face
had been ravaged by mustard gas in the trenches of the
Great War. The names of transgressors who breached school
rules were entered in a volume known as the Black Book.
Three entries in the book were punished with three strokes
of a bamboo cane.

The paedophiles included the Joint Headmaster, the
Chaplain and the Gamesmaster. Their attentions were

taken for granted and, not infrequently, encouraged by their victims.

These stark details may sound distressing, but I was not unhappy at Summer Fields. We enjoyed film nights at weekends, exeats on Sunday, swimming in the River Cherwell in the summer, boisterous rugby matches in the winter, and, joy of joys, the Hay Feast at harvest time, when the rule book was suspended and we were free to entomb the masters in stooks of hay and chaff.

It was in my final year that I first discovered *The Fellowship of the Ring*. The three volumes of J. R. R. Tolkien's *The Lord of The Rings* were first published in 1954 and 1955. I devoured all three by torchlight under the bedclothes. The images that these books printed on my mind remain even more vivid than those of the film versions made in New Zealand by Peter Jackson and released in 2001–03.

I came close to acquiring the right to publish the trilogy when the firm of Unwin Hyman came up for sale in 1990, but the prize was snatched by HarperCollins. I had to make do with a set of signed editions that were mauled by a dog and are now lost to history.

3. *The Lord of The Rings*

One Ring to rule them all,
one Ring to find them,
One Ring to bring them all,
and in the darkness bind them; …

J. R. R. Tolkien, epigraph to *The Lord of the Rings*

J. R. R.
TOLKIEN

THE
RETURN
OF THE
KING

Being the
Third Part
of
THE LORD
OF
THE RINGS

GEORGE ALLEN
AND UNWIN

J. R. R.
TOLKIEN

THE
TWO
TOWERS

Being the
Second Part
of
THE LORD
OF
THE RINGS

GEORGE ALLEN
AND UNWIN

J. R. R.
TOLKIEN

THE
FELLOWSHIP
OF THE
RING

Being the
First Part
of
THE LORD
OF
THE RINGS

GEORGE ALLEN
AND UNWIN

THE
FELLOWSHIP
OF THE RING

J. R. R. TOLKIEN

3

A King's Scholar at Eton
1956–61

Sis Bonus Puer
School motto: 'Be a good boy'

ooooo

In the autumn of 1955, I was awarded a scholarship to Eton
College. A year later I was inducted by the Provost to the
rituals of daily life. *Sis Bonus Puer, Docilis et Habilis* – Be
a good boy, ready and quick to learn. Our world was an
exquisite medieval microcosm, complete with a late Gothic
chapel, bell tower, refectory, cloisters and schoolhouse. The
seventy King's Scholars endowed in the fifteenth century
by King Henry VI donned black gowns over their school
uniforms, attended Chapel twice a day, and wore surplices
on Saints Days. All these rituals had been honed to perfection
by several hundred years of practice.

The other side of Eton high street was the domain of a
thousand or more Oppidans, the fee-paying majority, who
referred to the King's Scholars as tugs. (The nickname comes
from the Latin *togati*, meaning wearers of gowns.)

ooooo

Eton Microcosm, edited by Derek Anthony Parfit and Anthony Cheetham, was published by Sidgwick & Jackson in 1964. A miscellany of Eton's history and heritage, the book owes a great deal more to the creative genius of Derek Parfit than it does to any contribution of mine.

Derek was the number one scholar in my year. Over the next five years he won every prize for which he was eligible, and was awarded the top history scholarship to Balliol College, Oxford. I, meanwhile, did my best at Eton to be a good boy, ready and quick to learn. A number of outstanding teachers helped me along the way.

The Head Master, Robert Birley – a Balliol-educated historian whose liberal political opinions earned him the nickname 'Red Robert' – was occasionally called on to punish heinous breaches of school rules. In my case – I forget the nature of the crime – he commuted the statutory punishment and told me to write an essay on Galla Placidia, a woman I had never heard of before. I learned that she was the daughter of the Emperor Theodosius I, born in AD 388, married Ataulf, King of the Visigoths, was widowed by an assassin, then married the Emperor Constantius III, gave birth to the future Emperor Valentinian, and died in AD 450. She is commemorated in Ravenna by the magnificent Tomb of Galla Placidia, which bears her name but not her bones.

4. *Eton Microcosm*

Only two English Kings have gone completely insane.
Henry VI lost France, went mad and founded Eton.
George III petulantly disowned America, went mad
and became Eton's greatest benefactor.

From *Eton Microcosm*

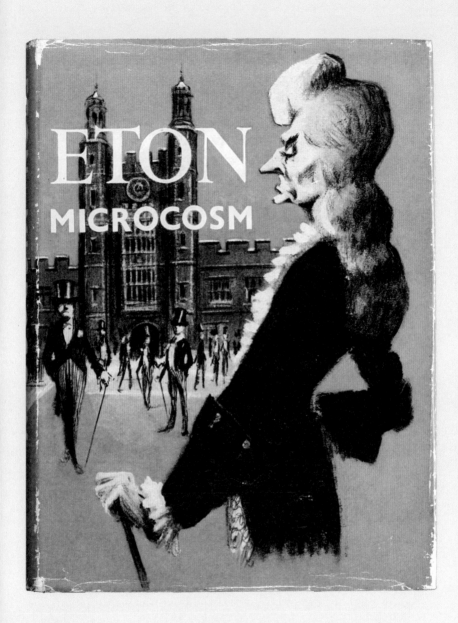

I was entirely enraptured. These tales from an era when Gothic warlords posed as emperors and imperial princesses were bartered as brides illumine the shadowlands between the end of Classical Antiquity and the start of the Middle Ages.

For my addiction to history I must also thank Ray Parry, a Welshman of contagious enthusiasm, who infected me with his passion for England's Civil Wars and Cromwell's Protectorate. I shed tears at his funeral when I saw how many others had gathered in College Chapel to remember his legacy.

During my five years as a King's Scholar, I saw little of my parents. Eton became my home. In 1956 my father was posted to Hungary as head of the British Legation in Budapest. When I visited Budapest that same year, in the immediate aftermath of the Hungarian Uprising, I found it a frightening and sinister city, its buildings scarred with bullet holes. When we ventured out of doors we were followed everywhere by men in flat caps and belted raincoats. The country's borders were ringed with a double line of barbed-wire fencing punctuated with watchtowers and defended by minefields. No one spoke a word of English and I could manage no more than a dozen words of Magyar.

Worse was to follow. My mother told me that she and my father were getting divorced. I took the first available flight back to England. At this low point I was deeply grateful to my Eton contemporary, Jonathan Aitken, and his family, who gave me a home from home at Playford Hall, their moated Tudor manor house in Suffolk.

Jonathan's father was Sir William Aitken, the Tory MP for Bury St Edmunds. A close neighbour was Winston's son, Randolph Churchill. Most weekends the house was filled with Tory grandees plotting to block Britain's accession to the Common Market or discussing the political and diplomatic debacle that followed the British-French-Israeli takeover of the Suez Canal.

ooooo

Three memories of Playford:

1. A prolonged duel on the croquet lawn with the Foreign Secretary, Selwyn Lloyd. We were both absurdly intent on winning the match. I eventually won by knocking his ball into the moat.

2. A Sunday lunch where Ted Heath was among the guests. I was acutely embarrassed by the way the grandees ignored a rising star in the Tory party and dismissed his views on closer ties with Europe.

3. But, most of all, the generosity and kindness of Jonathan's mother, Penelope, known as 'Pempe', who offered to fund the publication of *Eton Microcosm*, and made sure that her Masterchef, Mrs Carrier, kept me fed with feasts of my favourite dishes.

4

Balliol College, Oxford
1962–4

The Making of the Middle Ages

In the winter of 1962, Derek Parfit and I both sat the examination for a history scholarship to Balliol College, Oxford. This was a brave and possibly foolhardy decision. Only two scholarships were available, and Derek was almost certain to win one of them. He duly won the top history scholarship – the Brackenbury, named after a bequest from a Victorian philanthropist. I managed third place with a Domus Exhibition.

Derek and I shared tutorials on the French Revolution under the eye of Richard Cobb, an erudite left-wing maverick with a total disregard for convention (one obituary following his death in 1996 described Cobb as 'both an example of the scholarly life and a lord of misrule').

I chose the Early Middle Ages as my specialist subject in European History. This, too, was a brave decision: I knew nothing of the Middle Ages beyond the names of the kings and queens of England. But this ignorance was the very reason for my choice. Here was an opportunity to cross the English Channel and explore the Terra Incognita of the tenth and eleventh centuries, under expert guidance at a world-class university.

After passing Oxford's History Preliminary Examination, the first lecture I attended was delivered by Karl Leyser in the subterranean crypt of Magdalen College Chapel. Karl Leyser, an emigré from Nazi Germany with a gruff German accent, strode to the lectern, squared his shoulders, grasped his lapels and rasped: 'The first great empire of the Middle Ages was the empire of the Ottonian kings.' It was the most thrilling lecture I have heard, before or since. From that moment on I was sure that I had chosen the right subject.

Karl Leyser never completed the book that would surely have been his magnum opus: a definitive account of Germany's First Reich and the lives of the three Ottos who succeeded Henry the Fowler (king of East Francia, 919–936), the founding father of the Saxon dynasty.

Some years later, in 1993, I tried to fill the gap left by Professor Leyser's uncompleted work by publishing *An Embassy to Constantinople* by Liutprand of Cremona, a hard-hitting account by an Italian bishop of his diplomatic mission to the court of the Byzantine Emperor Nicephorus II Phocas in the year 968.

5. *An Embassy to Constantinople*

That the Ottos, the invincible auguſt emperors of the Romans and the moſt noble Adelaide, the auguſt empress, may always flourish, prosper and triumph, is the earneſt wish, desire and prayer of Liutprand bishop of the holy church of Cremona.

From the Epigraph, translated by F. A. Wright (1930)

PACE ET
BEL

LVITPRANDI
SVBDIACONI TOLETANI
TICINENSIS DIACONI
TANDEM CREMONENSIS EPISCOPI
OPERA QVÆ EXTANT.
CHRONICON ET ADVERSARIA
NVNC PRIMVM IN LVCEM EXEVNT.
P. HIERONYMI DE LA HIGVERA
SOCIET. IESV. PRESBYTERI
D. LAVRENTI RAMIREZ DE PRADO
CONSILIARII REGII
NOTIS ILLVSTRATA.

E. Quellinus delineavit.   Pet. Paul. Rubenius invenit.   Corn. Galleus iunior sculpsit.

ANTVERPIÆ, EX OFFICINA PLANTINIANA BALTHASARIS MORETI, M.DC.XL.

Liutprand was despatched by Otto I, known to history as Otto the Great, son of Henry the Fowler and the first ruler to be consecrated as Holy Roman Emperor since the death of Charlemagne. His objective was to settle a territorial dispute between East and West by marrying Otto's son and heir to a Byzantine princess named Theophanu.

The outcome was a fiasco: the Bishop and the Emperor met on 7 June 968. They loathed one another on sight. Liutprand returned empty-handed to Frankfurt. His unique legacy is this account of the summit meeting between the two superpowers of his day.

I left Oxford with a Second Class degree in History. This was a profoundly disappointing result. I felt – and still feel – that I let down not only myself but also some of the most inspiring history teachers at Eton and at Oxford.

5

A Year in Norway
1965

Working with Tibetan refugees for the Red Cross

At the end of January 1965, I went to Norway to teach English at a school for Tibetan refugees on a raspberry farm run by two lesbians and a sheepdog called Scott.

The farmhouse stood on a bluff overlooking a fjord on one side and bordered by pine-clad hills on the other. On the far side of the fjord lay the town of Kragerø in the province of Telemark, surrounded by forests, fjords and islands, and described by the painter Edvard Munch as the pearl among coastal towns.

I arrived in the bitter cold of midwinter. The day dawned at 10am and dusk closed in as early as 2pm in the afternoon. The neighbouring barns had two entrances, one at ground level for summer, and another in the attic for winter access, when snowdrifts covered the ground almost to the height of the building.

The weather was in stark contrast to the warmth with which I was welcomed. My arrival coincided with the state funeral of Winston Churchill, which took place on 30 January 1965. Churchill was revered in Norway as the bulldog who sent in the Royal Navy to recapture the strategically important port of Narvik in May 1940 and forged the wartime alliance between our two nations. My first duty on arrival was to address a public meeting in Kragerø's town hall on the life and legacy of the great man. The meeting was packed to the gunwales, not, I suspect, because I had anything interesting to say, but owing to the courtesy, friendliness and goodwill of the people of Norway.

The seventeen Tibetan teenagers in my care lived and worked in a converted barn house. The spartan schoolroom was furnished with seventeen mats on the floor and a blackboard on the wall. The library comprised a single copy of the *Concise Oxford Dictionary*. I spoke not a word of Tibetan. My charges knew no English. Neither they nor I understood Norwegian. But they were supremely motivated. In their free time they ransacked the dictionary for new words with which they could ambush me on the following day.

Towards the end of my stint as a teacher, I sent some of the essays written by my star pupil, Sonam Tobgyal, to the Master of Balliol and asked if the College would consider awarding him a scholarship. The college was prepared to do so, but the idea was rejected by the Red Cross on the grounds that it would be wrong to select a single member of the school for special treatment.

During the month of May, the Norwegian countryside is transformed by an annual miracle. At the start of the month it still lies under a blanket of snow and there are ice sheets in the fjord. By the end of May the snow has vanished. The sun rises at three in the morning, there are swimmers in the fjord, the sea is dotted with white sails, cascades of sparkling snow water come down from the hills, and the sun remains high in the sky until ten o'clock at night.

At the end of my working day I would climb up into

the hills with a good book for company and gaze out over the pristine forests, fjords and islands admired by Edvard Munch.

The Magic Mountain was my favourite companion. It was among the books sent to me by Peter Buckman, a Balliol contemporary, who had found a job at Penguin Books. It tells the story of Hans Castorp, a young German from Hamburg who travels to visit his cousin in a Swiss alpine sanatorium for the victims of tuberculosis.

During his visit, Hans discovers that he too has a patch on his lungs. He remains in the sanatorium for seven years until he enlists in the German army to fight for his country in the Great War. He accepts that in all probability he will die on the battlefield. During his prolonged rest cure, Castorp meets a number of characters who represent the ideologies that were influential in Europe in the era before the First World War. First published in 1929, it is not the greatest of Mann's works, but a masterpiece nonetheless, and an elegy to life in the face of death.

Peter's generosity in sending me books played an important part in my decision to find a job in publishing when I returned from Norway.

6. *The Magic Mountain*

An unassuming young man was travelling,
in midsummer, from his native city of Hamburg
to Davos-Platz in the Canton of the Grisons
on a three weeks' visit.

Opening sentence of *The Magic Mountain*,
translated by H. T. Lowe-Porter (1927)

Thomas Mann

———

Der
Zauberberg

Erster Band

Thomas Mann

———

Der
Zauberberg

Zweiter Band

6

The New English Library
1966–8

My first job in publishing

I landed my first job in publishing on a chilly November day in 1966. When I proudly told my father that I was now employed at a salary of £1,200 per annum, he was profoundly disappointed that I hadn't chosen, as he had, a career as a public servant. I pointed out that they were actually paying me to read books. I thought then, as I believe now, that publishing is a passport to roam across the entire spectrum of human experience, endeavour and belief.

The New English Library was an American-owned paperback publisher with offices in Holborn. It was run by two men who had nothing in common other than an addiction to gambling.

Gareth Powell was the son of a Welsh coal miner. Christopher Shaw was a wealthy upper-crust banker. Together they plundered the US bestseller lists, acquiring UK paperback rights. Their most notable success was *The Carpetbaggers* (1961) by Harold Robbins, the author of twenty-five bestsellers with worldwide sales of 750 million copies in thirty-two languages. Under their tutelage I had my first lessons in the art of the deal.

My first ever acquisition was the paperback rights in Frank Herbert's classic science-fiction saga, *Dune* (1965). It was a lucky accident. At the end of my first week as a junior editor, Gareth strode into the editorial office with a hefty typescript under his arm and asked whether any one of us read science fiction. I volunteered at once.

I didn't mention that I'd already read *Dune* during my year in Norway – not the whole book, but the abridged serialisation that had appeared in the science-fiction magazine *Analog.*

The New English Library bought the UK paperback rights for the princely advance of £1,100. It has now been reprinted at least fifty times and is said to be the bestselling science-fiction novel of all time.

Two film adaptations have also left their mark on millions more who are not science fiction readers. *Dune* spawned a series of sequels, but none of them equals this introduction to a far-future galactic civilisation of a thousand worlds, ruled by an abominably perverted emperor, and liberated by the genetically modified messiah who controls the life-giving spice emitted by gargantuan worms under the desert sands of Arrakis.

7. *Dune*

Unique among SF novels. I know nothing
comparable to it except *The Lord of the Rings.*

Arthur C. Clarke

FRANK
HERBERT
DUNE

NEW ENGLISH LIBRARY

7

Sphere Books
1969–72

Hired and fired
by the Thomson organisation

In 1969 I was recruited as a junior editor at Sphere Books. The Managing Director was Richard B. Fischer, a mild-mannered American academic who had come to England to fly long-range B26 bombing missions in the dying days of the Third Reich. His mission at Sphere Books was to start a paperback publishing imprint within the publishing empire of the Canadian entrepreneur Roy Thomson, who also owned *The Sunday Times* and a raft of well-established UK book publishers: Hamish Hamilton, Michael Joseph and Thomas Nelson.

I was given a great deal of latitude for one so junior and inexperienced, and I made a number of hideous mistakes. I turned down the paperback rights in David Niven's autobiography *The Moon's a Balloon* (1971), which went on to sell more than two million copies. I rejected James Herriot's *All Creatures Great and Small*, the stories of his experiences as a Yorkshire vet, which became the most lucrative franchise of the decade. Lord Thomson rang me in person, however, to tell me that he could not condone the publication of *The Happy Hooker* (1971), the autobiography of a Dutch prostitute, which had stirred a flurry of prurient interest from the tabloid press.

In 1970 Sphere published the paperback edition of *Grapefruit*, a book of poems by Yoko Ono, with an introduction by her husband, John Lennon. This set the stage for my first encounter with a world-class celebrity.

We arranged a book signing to take place at Selfridges at nine o'clock in the morning. There was no prior announcement or press briefing of the event. A stretch limo delivered our authors on time outside the store. The moment John Lennon stepped out onto the pavement there was an outbreak of mass hysteria.

The entire ground floor of Selfridges had been cleared out in anticipation of the signing. By the time John and Yoko sat down at a table stacked high with copies of *Grapefruit*, the room was packed with fans and the outer doors had to be barred for safety reasons.

In the allotted hour we sold some 2,000 signed copies. There was no way our authors could keep up with demand. Along with Sphere's press officer, I was co-opted to imitate the signatures of our authors in the books we were selling. More than fifty years later, I owe an apology to the victims of this act of forgery.

I was not held to account for this or any other of my mistakes, though. My demise at Sphere Books was brought about by a wholly improbable case of mistaken identity. Sphere had reported disappointing results. A man named Don Teasdale was recruited as managing director to turn the company around. Teasdale had an impressive CV as the former MD of Weidenfeld & Nicolson. But it gradually became clear to the staff at Sphere that Teasdale was not who he appeared to be. He knew little about books, was habitually drunk from lunchtime onwards, and he never told the truth when a lie would do. I was elected by my colleagues to share our misgivings with my boss at Thomson HQ, George Rainbird, a distinguished book packager who had recently sold his business to Roy Thomson. George heard me out and assured me that he had personally checked out Teasdale's credentials and found no traces of improper behaviour.

Back at Sphere we were not one whit reassured: Teasdale's behaviour grew worse, to the point where none of us would venture to speak to him when he returned to the office at 4pm after his lunch. I made a final appeal to Geoffrey Parrack, George Rainbird's boss at Thomson's. When George heard of this, he knew that he had to fire me for an unforgivable breach of protocol. But he also recognised that we shared an interest in Egypt's boy pharaoh, Tutankhamen. His greatest success as a packager was Christiane Desroches Noblecourt's *Tutankhamen* (1963), a momentous international bestseller inspired by the centenary exhibition of Howard Carter's discovery.

George Rainbird was actually quite reluctant to fire me. He gave me brownie points for republishing Howard Carter's own account of the discovery, *The Tomb of Tutankhamun*, first published in three volumes between 1923 and 1927. It was therefore a very civilised sacking, delivered at the lunch table of a smart West End restaurant and washed down with a bottle of first-growth claret.

Don Teasdale did eventually meet his come-uppance. He was caught with his fingers in the till and sacked for fraud and embezzlement. I never found out whether he was a professional con man who assumed the name of Teasdale or a troubled schizophrenic driven mad by drink and drugs.

Confessions of a Window Cleaner (1971) by Timothy Lea was Sphere's first national bestseller; it became a hit movie and spawned a host of sequels with sales numbered in the millions. Timothy Lea was not the author's real name, but a pseudonym adopted by Christopher Wood, an author who came to play an important role in my life over the next forty years.

Under his own name, Christopher had written a semi-autobiographical first novel, *Make It Happen To Me* (1969), about his postgraduate experiences in Africa with VSO (Voluntary Service Overseas). He and I first met when I bought the paperback rights of this novel. He told me that his net earnings from the book, following the expenses of a threatened libel action, were £120, and asked whether I had any ideas about how he could make a living from his writing. I invited him to lunch at the Ritz in Piccadilly.

Thus was born the name and character of Timothy Lea, a cheeky, cheerful window cleaner, who peered from his ladder to witness the manners, morals and sexual proclivities of his middle-class customers on the far side of the glass. Sterner critics might call this soft porn, but I would argue that Lea's adventures exhibit more than a touch of genius.

Nineteen seventy-three was the year in which we launched the Abacus paperbacks imprint, under the slogan

8. *Confessions of a Window Cleaner*

It always took longer to clean the inside of the windows.
Viv preferred a man with experience.
Dorothy was a little careless with her underclothes.
Mrs Armstrong provided tea and cake beforehand.
Brenda consumed marshmallows afterwards.
Overwhelmed by the hospitality of his customers
Tim found it difficult to keep his mind on the job.

From the back-cover blurb

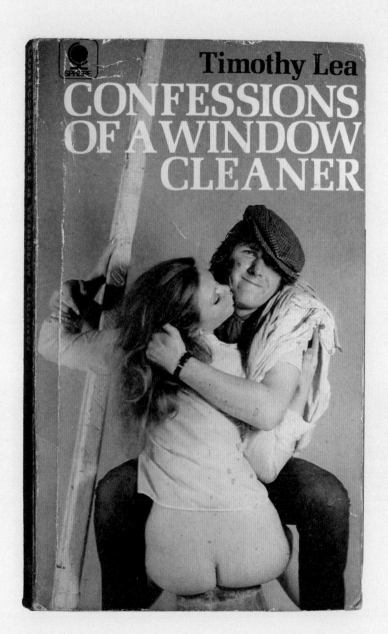

Timothy Lea

CONFESSIONS
OF A WINDOW
CLEANER

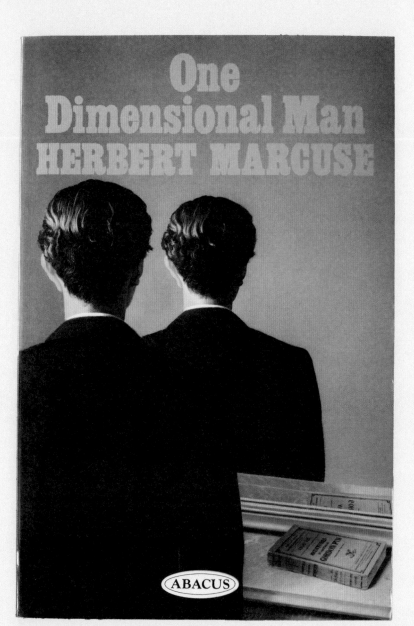

'Books that Count'. It was my first effort at creating and naming a new imprint. It is still extant and active as part of the Hachette Publishing Group.

The books we published under the Abacus logo were an exotic mix of serious scholarship and downright battiness. I remain particularly fond of the batty books: they testify to my belief that there is no opinion so inane or insane that it doesn't attract a following. Flying saucers, alien visitations, lost continents, psychic powers, doomsday prophecies and colliding planets: these are among the treats in store for readers of Immanuel Velikovsky's *Worlds In Collision* and *Earth In Upheaval*, John Michell's *The View Over Atlantis*, Charles Fort's *The Book Of The Damned*, Sheila Ostrander and Lynn Schroeder's *Psychic Discoveries Behind The Iron Curtain*, and John A. Keel's *UFOs: Operation Trojan Horse*.

All of these were featured in the Abacus catalogue for 1973, side by side with works of serious history, philosophy and media studies that have stood the test of time. Marshall McLuhan's *Understanding Media* (1968), for example, is a pioneering history of the communications industry from the invention of the printing press to the electronic era. *The Conquest of The Incas* (1972) by John Hemming, meanwhile, is a mammoth and definitive account of one the cruellest

9. *One-Dimensional Man*

The capabilities (intellectual and material) of contemporary society are immeasurably greater than ever before – which means that the scope of society's domination over the individual is immeasurably greater than ever before.

Herbert Marcuse

episodes in colonial history, and Kate Millett's *Sexual Politics* (1972) is recognised as a foundation stone of second-wave feminism.

One-Dimensional Man, first published in 1964, is a Marxist critique of modern capitalism written by a professor of philosophy at the University of California. Herbert Marcuse's book is a scathing attack on the evils of technological capitalism as a form of totalitarian control and on the consumer capitalism of the USA in particular. It was adopted as a manifesto and a call to arms by the student activists who took to the streets of Paris in May 1968.

At the invitation of Edward Mortimer, an Oxford contemporary and *Times* reporter who was covering these events at the point when student protest was turning to revolutionary violence, I spent a memorable night in a Parisian taxi, speeding from one flashpoint to the next as he wrote his copy. The taxi driver unleashed a barrage of colourful swear words, and I wondered whether I was witnessing the downfall of de Gaulle and the Fifth Republic.

Edward Mortimer was a good friend throughout our time at Summer Fields and at Balliol. Like Derek Parfit, he won every academic accolade on offer, top scholarships to Eton and Balliol, a congratulatory first at Oxford and a Life Fellowship at All Souls. He spent most of his subsequent career in New York as a senior adviser to the United Nations and was the author of a clutch of authoritative books on subjects ranging from French history to the politics of Islam.

In 1972 I was commissioned by Weidenfeld & Nicolson to write a short book on *The Life and Times of Richard III*. It was to be part of a series on the Kings and Queens of England, edited by Antonia Fraser and published by Book Club Associates for members of their History Book Club. I was the odd man out, given that most of the authors were well-established academic historians. The reason I got the job was that I promised to deliver my 40,000-word text within three months. I was promised a flat fee of £750.

My editor, Christopher Falkus, kept watch on my progress with regular lunches at a transport café in the Camberwell New Road, where you could get a bacon sandwich for just 10p. Since I already had a busy day job at Sphere Books, I wrote the book after dark, according to a strict timetable: start typing at 10pm, bedtime at 2am, then back at the office by 9.30am the following morning.

I delivered on time. The Kings and Queens series proved to be a massive success, and I was given an ex-gratia bonus of £250 a year later. But more important in the long term was the entrée it gave me to the world of George Weidenfeld and his star author, Antonia Fraser.

My research for the book also introduced me to the late fifteenth-century origins of the British publishing industry. In 1476 William Caxton set up his printing press at the Almonry in Westminster. Among his earliest bestsellers was an anthology entitled *Dictes and Sayengis of the Philosophres* (1477). A spring tide of bestsellers was to follow: Ovid's *Metamorphoses*, Aesop's *Fables*, Chaucer's *Canterbury Tales*, a *History of Troy* and Malory's *Le Morte d'Arthur* (1485).

The typography, the illuminations and the vibrant colours of Caxton's books are in themselves a joy and a wonder. They testify to the reverence paid to books at the dawning of the age of Gutenberg.

10. *The Life and Times of Richard III*

Now is the winter of our discontent
Made glorious summer by this sun of York; ...

William Shakespeare, *Richard III,* Act I, Scene III

The Life and Times of
RICHARD III
Anthony Cheetham

General Editor: Antonia Fraser

Futura presents Futura in the 80's.

8

Futura Publications
1973–81
Cowboys in Camberwell

On leaving Sphere Books, I was recruited by The British Printing Corporation to launch a new paperback company under the name of Futura, as part of the BPC's publishing arm, known as Macdonald & Co.

The man who entrusted me with this mission was Monty Alfred, the Commercial Director, and later the Chairman, of our parent company. He had no background or experience in the book business but treated me with memorable kindness and implicit trust.

Futura was our name. The Shape of Books to Come was our slogan. We rented offices and a warehouse behind the bus station on the Camberwell New Road. Futura was the only British publishing house with offices south of the river. We saw ourselves as the Camberwell Cowboys, unfettered by convention and free to roam where others feared to tread.

The cowboys made an impressive start. Christopher Wood, aka Timothy Lea, joined us from Sphere with his *Confessions* series and recruited new writers with a taste for bedroom antics. These included *The Confessions of a Night Nurse* (1974) by Rosie Dixon, a pseudonym for Justin Cartwright, one of whose later – more serious – works would be shortlisted for the Booker Prize.

We sold a million copies of *Rugby Songs* (1967), a mildly pornographic miscellany of locker-room drinking songs.

We launched a new imprint, Troubadour Spectaculars, to publish steamy historical romances from America: *Sweet Savage Love* (1974) by Rosemary Rogers, *The Flame and The Flower* (1972) by Kathleen Woodiwiss, and *Love's Tender Fury* (1976) by Jennifer Wilde.

We invented the Kung Fu Western as a vehicle for the adventures of *Sloane, Fastest Fist in the West* (1974).

SS Panzer Battalion (1975) was the first in a sequence of novels recounting the fortunes of an elite German tank unit from Dunkirk to Kursk, and from Normandy to the Ardennes. Their author was Leo Kessler, one of a number of pseudonyms of the remarkably prolific military historian Charles Whiting.

All of these series were first published in paperback and designated for distribution through the mass market – CTNs (Confectioners, Tobacconists, and News retailers), corner shops, airports and railway stations and the wholesalers who serviced them. We were, however, equally ambitious to develop our company as a publisher at the serious end

11. *Alexander the Great*

A magnificent, compelling epic. He discovers the most
extraordinary king and general of Antiquity, the last Homeric
hero. He has honoured him splendidly.

The Sunday Telegraph

ROBIN LANE FOX
ALEXANDER
THE GREAT

The Choirboys

JOSEPH WAMBAUGH

A novel by the author of
THE ONION FIELD

of the market. The British Printing Corporation sanctioned the upgrade in our ambitions and we duly upped our game.

We published the paperback edition of Robin Lane Fox's first book, *Alexander the Great*, in 1975, when the author was a lecturer at Worcester College, Oxford. He has been a titan of classical history ever since.

He is also an intrepid horseman and an omniscient botanist who writes a weekly gardening column in the *Financial Times*. He once interviewed me in his column, under the headline 'A Mogul of Trees', probably the finest job title of my lifetime.

Robin is a neighbour of mine in the Cotswolds. We meet at lunches and dinners, where he talks knowledgeably on any subject under the sun. My garden near Chipping Campden is a showcase for the exotic salvias he has kindly donated as cuttings. But I value him most for his life of Alexander, the man who was tutored by Aristotle, gave his name to fifteen cities from the river Nile to the Hindu Kush, and wept when his generals declined to let him conquer the world.

In 1976 I was introduced to the crime novels of Joseph Wambaugh. Joe was a man of many talents, a former Sergeant in the US Marine Corps, an officer in the Los Angeles Police Department and the author of a string of outstanding crime

12. *The Choirboys*

… the importance of [Wambaugh's] best fiction…
is amplified by his unequalled ability to capture the nuances
of the LAPD's isolated and essentially Hobbesian
tribal culture.

Tim Rutten, *Los Angeles Times*

stories set in a hard-boiled world of cops who bend the law as well as enforcing it. For me the most memorable of these is *The Choirboys*, a comedy drama about a group of LA police officers who unwind at night by holding drinking sessions in a local park. The novel was catapulted into the bestseller lists by the Robert Aldrich movie version, released in 1977.

Joe's books remained part of my life over many years. Thirty-six years later we published *Harbour Nocturne* (2013) at Head of Zeus (the company I had launched the previous year). We had a minor spat about the title: Joe insisted, rightly, that we should have used the American spelling – Harbor, not Harbour. I apologised, and he replied with an invitation to visit him at his home in San Diego. *Mi casa*, he said, *es tu casa*. The real treasure of a life in books is the memory of authors such as Joe Wambaugh.

Ken Follett's Second World War spy thriller *Storm Island* was born on the top deck of a number 46 bus. I was supposed to be interviewing him for a job as Sales Director at Futura, but wound up by offering him a two-book contract and an advance of £3,000.

The story is set in 1944 on a fictitious island in the Hebrides, where Henry Faber, a German master spy charged with reporting Allied plans for the D-Day landings, has taken refuge.

Ken allowed me to introduce a twist in the plot. Faber's landlady on the island has an affair with him and works out

13. *Storm Island*

An absolutely terrific thriller, so pulse-pounding,
so ingenious in its plotting and so frighteningly realistic
that you simply cannot stop reading.

From the review in *Publishers Weekly*

STORM ISLAND

KEN FOLLETT

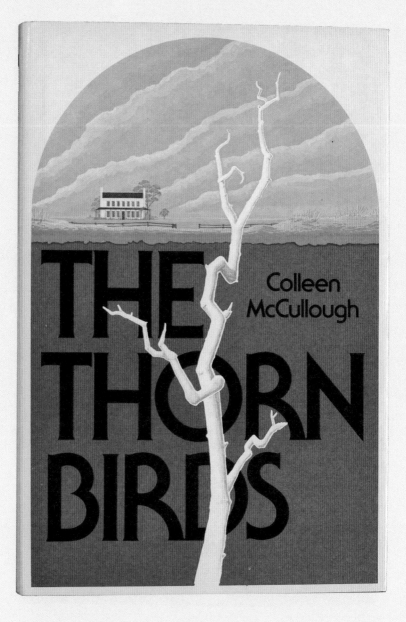

Colleen McCullough

THE THORN BIRDS

that he is, in fact, a German spy. She must therefore make a choice between the man she loves and her duty to king and country.

Before the novel was published in the UK, the US rights were sold at auction in New York for $800,000, and the book was retitled *Eye of the Needle*. When Ken phoned me at home on a Sunday morning, my heart sank. I knew at once that the minuscule advance of £1,500 that I had paid out for an international bestseller would preclude any further deals with the cowboys in Camberwell. He did, nonetheless, deliver *Triple* (1979), the second novel in our contract, before he went on to become a superstar with his *Pillars of the Earth* sequence.

Futura's megaton hardcover breakthrough arrived on the wings of Colleen McCullough's novel *The Thorn Birds* in 1977. We had to offer the author a very large advance, but our investment paid handsome dividends, as the book went on to sell more than 30 million copies around the world. It also spawned a lifelong friendship between the publisher and author.

Futura acquired the UK rights to *The Thorn Birds* in a protracted auction that dragged on for several weeks and

14. *The Thorn Birds*

There is a legend about a bird that sings just once in its life, more sweetly than any other creature on the face of the earth. From the moment it leaves the nest it searches for a thorn tree and does not rest until it has found one. Then it impales itself upon the longest, sharpest spine. And dying, it rises above its own agony to out-carol the lark and the nightingale. One superlative song, existence the price. But the whole world listens... For the best is only bought at the cost of great pain.

Excerpt from the author's Preface

ended at midnight on a Sunday. Our rivals were Transworld, who were every bit as determined as we were to secure the rights. We eventually agreed on a procedure known as the 'sudden death' auction, where the participants agree a deadline for final offers and the best offer wins the rights.

I did not ask my chairman, Monty Alfred, for his permission before I put in our winning bid of £655,000. I was afraid that he might refuse to do so and preferred to risk his displeasure rather than risk losing the auction. It says a great deal for both his tolerance and his business acumen that he sanctioned the deal after the fact without demur.

The Thorn Birds is a romance about a sheep farmer's daughter in New South Wales who falls in love with a Roman Catholic priest. Their passion is consummated on a tropical island hideaway. She returns to the farm; he is called to Rome and elevated to become a Cardinal.

In short, it is an adolescent fantasy with an absurd story-line. But it enjoyed astonishing global success, becoming the best-selling book in Australian history and generating a multiple Emmy-winning TV mini-series and even a musical.

Almost everything its author did was writ larger than life. Colleen made her home in Norfolk Island, a remote outcrop in the South Pacific halfway between Queensland and Auckland. She married Ric Robinson, the islander who built her home. She filled her home with exquisite paintings by Sidney Nolan and other leading Australian artists. Here she held court, entertained visitors and embarked on a massive series of novels, *Masters of Rome*, based on the life and times of Julius Caesar. She wrote several thousand words a day and published some thirty books before she passed away in 2015. Her last book was titled *Life Without the Boring Bits* (2011). Over a period of three decades I was a regular guest at her Norfolk Island estate and she made periodic visits to mine in the Cotswolds.

Her hospitality was as legendary as her writing. During the daytime she remained incommunicado at her typewriter. At dusk she would descend to the kitchen in her pinafore and cook up gargantuan feasts of roast meat and sweet potatoes, washed down with flagons of Wolf Blass Red Label Shiraz Cabernet. In the small hours she would challenge her guests to marathons at the Scrabble board.

ooooo

I got hold of a copy of Dan O'Bannon's screenplay for *Alien* (1979) before the film was released and felt that the storyline alone was a masterpiece of science fiction, horror and suspense.

We acquired the rights to publish the novelisation of the film, written by the US science-fiction writer Alan Dean Foster. This led to an invitation from Twentieth Century Fox to a preview at their studios in Hollywood. The screening theatre had been decorated for a prior VIP screening with the grotesquely beautiful set designs of Hans Rudi Giger.

I couldn't watch the whole movie, either then or since, without closing my eyes at the terror points. But I fell in love with Sigourney Weaver, I venerate Ridley Scott, and we sold well over a million copies of Alan Dean Foster's novel.

15. *Alien*

In space no one can hear you scream.

The tag line of the advertising campaign
for Ridley Scott's film

Presents

ALIEN

ALAN DEAN FOSTER

In space
no one can hear you
scream.

THE CLASSIC
FILM OF ULTIMATE
TERROR

9

Working for Robert Maxwell
1981–2
Czech mate

One morning in July 1981 the news broke that Robert Maxwell had launched a dawn raid on the London Stock Exchange and secured a controlling stake in the shares of the British Printing Corporation.

Already known as the Bouncing Czech, Maxwell was a Jewish refugee who had made his way to England, changed his name from Jan Hoch and enlisted as an officer in the British army. It was also known that he had a monstrous ego, unlimited ambitions and a longstanding feud with his rival press baron, Rupert Murdoch.

I assured my colleagues at Macdonald Futura that we had nothing to worry about. Our company was just one of thirty-five subsidiaries within BPC. Our new overlord, therefore, would be barely aware of our existence.

Not so. Over the next three years barely a day passed without a meeting or a phone call with the Bouncing Czech. Maxwell had boundless energy and an insatiable drive to take the lead in every decision, great or small, across his media empire. He would treat me, according to his mood, either as a courtier or a confidant, as a sounding board or a punchbag.

Maxwell may well have been an ogre and a bully, but he was also a committed Zionist, a playful charmer and a devoted father. He had a formidable intellect and a lively sense of humour. I began to look forward to our meetings. Maxwell was often grumpy, always challenging, but never boring.

He took a childlike pleasure in the new set of toys he found at the British Printing Corporation. Abandoned print factories and crumbling warehouses were magically transformed, in his mind, into helicopter pads and gleaming skyscrapers. He gave me a guided tour of his headquarters at Headington Hill Hall in Oxford, the inner sanctum that housed the scientific journals of the Pergamon Press. He explained to me in detail his plans to replace Rupert Murdoch as Britain's premier media mogul and to transform the Pergamon Press into the world's leading academic textbook publisher.

16. *Cosmos*

The Cosmos was discovered only yesterday. For a million years it was clear to everyone that there were no other places than the Earth. Then in the last tenth of a percent of the lifetime of our species we reluctantly noticed that... we lived on a tiny and fragile world lost in immensity and eternity, drifting in a great cosmic ocean, dotted here and there with a hundred billion galaxies and a billion million stars.

Excerpt from Chapter 13, entitled 'Who Speaks For Earth?'

COSMOS
CARL SAGAN

I was never bored, but was ultimately overwhelmed. The mood changed dramatically at Macdonald Futura when the National Union of Journalists went on strike to protest against Maxwell's proposed redundancies, occupied our offices, and picketed the entrance to deter management from entering the building. The lockout lasted several weeks (and engendered at least three unplanned pregnancies among the occupants). The NUJ also published daily instalments of a graphic novel in which I was lampooned as the Mekon, an evil little green man from the planet Venus.

Along with six of my senior colleagues at Macdonald Futura, I decided the time was right to jump ship and set about the launch of a new company – of which more in the next chapter.

A footnote: the final enigma in the life of Robert Maxwell is the one posed by his death from drowning in the early hours of 5 November 1991. Did he fall, was he pushed, or did he commit suicide? I suspect the answer owes more to common sense than to forensics. Maxwell knew that the game was up. He had been exposed as the man who stole hundreds of millions from the pension funds of the Mirror Group to shore up his other companies. His most prized asset, the Pergamon Press, had already gone. It was only a matter of time before his friends in Israel denied him the privilege of burial on the Mount of Olives outside Jerusalem. He had to take his life then and there, and he did so.

ooooo

Carl Sagan introduced me to the realm of astrophysics. He was an immensely distinguished American professor, a prize-winning writer, and the author of some thirty books.

Cosmos is both an ode to the wonders of the universe and a bridge between science fact and science fiction. In Sagan's company, the discoveries of the astronomers seem every bit as awesome as the imagined starscapes of the world's best science-fiction writers. *Cosmos* is a journey through time and space. In thirteen chapters the author walks the reader inwards from the furthest reaches of the galaxy to the origin myths of humankind.

We published *Cosmos* in a generous format illustrated with hundreds of photographs, to coincide with a thirteen-part TV series that claimed 400 million viewers across sixty countries. There is an image in *Cosmos* that springs to mind every time I open a book on the mysteries of time and space. Sagan asks the reader to compare the size of the nucleus in a single atom to that of a dust mote suspended in the nave of a medieval cathedral.

10

Century Publishing
1982–5

A new start with a happy ending

Century Publishing made an uncertain start. There were only two of us, Gail Rebuck and myself. We had no offices, no money, and no name. We set up camp in premises provided free of charge in the offices of Ward Lock. We sought funding from a Hong Kong Chinese entrepreneur named Au Bak Ling, who turned us down when he saw that one of the books in our prospectus was called *A Dark and Distant Shore*. Very bad luck, he murmured. The gossip columnist in *Publishing News* caught hold of the story and renamed him Ai Back Out.

We eventually found a venture capital firm, Venture Link, who lent us the money to get started, and moved into modest quarters next to a wine shop in Old Compton Street. We were by now a team of seven and agreed to name the company Orion, after the Greek myth of the mighty hunter in the constellation of Orion, with a shield in the right hand and a sword in the left. Unfortunately, we were told that the name was already registered by a bank. I had to wait another nine years for the mighty hunter. We settled instead for Century Publishing.

The next three years proved to be very profitable indeed. Everything we touched seemed to turn to gold. We moved into smart offices in Soho's Wedgwood Mews and held our monthly board meetings in the Escargot restaurant on the other side of Greek Street.

Light A Penny Candle (1982) by Maeve Binchy was the first book we published under the Century imprint. The novel was named after a racehorse that my senior colleague (and second wife) Rosie de Courcy spotted in the racing pages of the *Evening Standard*. I don't know how the horse fared, but the book romped home as a number-one bestseller.

Maeve Binchy's novels made an enormous contribution, not just at Century, but further down the track, when she followed Rosie and me to the Orion Publishing Group. She was, by this time, a bestseller on both sides of the Atlantic, fêted not just in Dublin and in London but also in Chicago and New York.

The passage of time has also elevated her status as a writer. It was recognised that her writing was deceptively simple, camouflaging a subtle and sophisticated insight into motive and character. Her novels now feature in the Irish secondary-school curriculum and she has a garden dedicated to her at the Irish Museum of Literature in Dublin. Maeve was the first Irish writer to achieve worldwide success on such an unimaginable scale. I was no more than a spectator at these events, but it would be churlish to ignore the impact of Maeve's sales on the fortunes of our companies.

Century's most successful non-fiction publication was our single-volume abridgement of three books first published by Oxford University Press between 1939 and 1943: *Lark Rise*, *Over to Candleford* and *Candleford Green*. Flora Thompson was a self-taught writer who set out to recapture the idylls of an Oxfordshire country childhood in the Victorian era.

I took the idea of an illustrated edition to a book packager, Julian Shuckburgh, who came back with the most beautiful presentations we had ever seen: a cloth-bound cover with a printed label, a text scattered with leaves, flowers, birds and questing wildlife, and sheaves of full-page Victorian landscape paintings by leading artists of the nineteenth century.

The Illustrated Lark Rise to Candleford was an instant number-one bestseller. Book Club Associates ordered 120,000 copies as a Main Selection, and the book remained on the bestseller list for the best part of a year. Other illustrated country classics followed: Flora Thompson's *Still Glides the Stream* (1984), Laurie Lee's *Cider With Rosie* (1984), Richard Mabey's *The Frampton Flora* (1985) and *Kilvert's Diary* (1986) by Francis Kilvert.

Gail Rebuck also introduced a programme of New Age manuals on health, diet, exercise and mental well-being. Her books tapped into a new generation of readers who had no experience of the hardships and privations of wartime Britain. Her foremost lifestyle guru was Leslie Kenton, author of *The Joy of Beauty* and *Raw Energy* (1984). Her vegetarian recipes and natural cosmetics were not my cup of tea, but I did my best not to show it.

In 1985 Gail married Philip Gould, the pollster who later rebranded the Labour Party as New Labour and transformed the prospects of its leader, Tony Blair. He also masterminded Gail's rise to the apex of British publishing.

Gould was excellent company: witty, mischievous and not averse to strong drink. One evening he took us out to dinner at a West End nightclub, the Zanzibar, and challenged me to see which of us could do the greater number of press-ups on the dance floor.

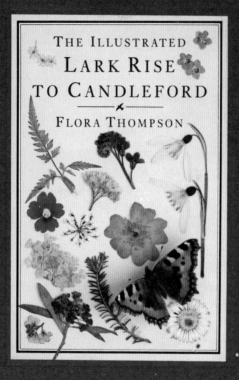

THE ILLUSTRATED
LARK RISE
TO CANDLEFORD

FLORA THOMPSON

The price of losing the bet, as I did, was that I should let Gail take over from Rosie de Courcy as the grande dame of Century Publishing. I later discovered that he was not joking.

∞∞∞

The Century Travellers is a library of 200 books devoted to the explorers and adventurers, soldiers and spies, pilgrims and eccentrics, tourists and sightseers who brought the world to their armchair readers back at home. I was closely involved in choosing the books. All of them are my favourites, but here are four with a special magic.

On Sledge and Horseback To the Outcast Siberian Lepers (1893), by the Victorian missionary and explorer Kate Marsden, is the book with the most beguiling title. It was said at the time that her mission to Siberia was a self-imposed penance for her lesbian orientation. Russia's Tsarina provided her with a letter of commendation on her three-year-round trip of 11,000 miles.

For her tenth birthday, Dervla Murphy was given a second-hand bicycle and a second-hand atlas. In 1963 she set out for India on a man's bicycle that included a pistol

17. *The Illustrated Lark Rise to Candleford*

The hamlet stood on a gentle rise in the flat, wheat-growing north-east corner of Oxfordshire. We will call it Lark Rise because of the great number of skylarks which made the surrounding fields their springboard and nested on the bare earth between the rows of green corn.

The opening lines of *Lark Rise to Candleford*

in its kit. She eventually arrived in Delhi, recorded her numerous misadventures en route and posted her book to an eminent publisher in London. *Full Tilt*, first published in 1965, was the first of seventeen books that described her rides to seventeen different countries.

Freya Stark was the peerless explorer of Araby and Persia between the wars. In 1983 we republished her most acclaimed book, *The Southern Gates of Arabia* (originally published in 1936), on the day of her ninetieth birthday. Her journey across the bleak and arid Hadramaut marked an extraordinary achievement for a European woman travelling without an armed escort in a region contested by rival Bedouin tribes.

A. F. Tschiffely's enchanting *Southern Cross to Pole Star* is a singular model of humanity, modesty and charm. Aimé Tschiffely was a Swiss schoolteacher who emigrated to Argentina, where he acquired two feral pampas horses, whom he named Mancho and Gato (Spot and Cat).

In the mid-1920s, he made a bet that he could ride Mancho and Gato from Buenos Aires to Washington, DC, a journey of some ten thousand miles. Tschiffely's epic ride took him three years, from 1925 to 1928. His exploits were taken up by the press and many thousands gathered to cheer him on his way. In 1998, more than four decades after his death and in accordance with a proviso in his will, his ashes were buried on a Patagonian farm alongside those of his four-legged companions.

18. *Southern Cross to Pole Star*

A ride which beats all the great rides
of history clean out of the field.

The Times

A.F. Tschiffely
SOUTHERN CROSS
TO POLE STAR
Introduction by Eric Newby

II

Century Hutchinson
1985–9
The minnow that swallowed a whale

The Frankfurt Book Fair in October 1985 was the scene of a meeting that transformed the fortunes of Century's founders and opened a new chapter in my career. The man responsible was Christopher Bland, the Chair of London Weekend Television. LWT were the owners of Hutchinson & Co., one of Britain's leading publishing groups. We were introduced because Hutchinson handled warehousing and distribution services for Century Publishing.

Christopher knew that Century had made an impressive start and asked me about our plans for the future. I told him we still had a long way to go and added, on the spur of the moment, that we would be happy to make a bid for Hutchinson if the opportunity were to arise. He smiled politely and left. But later in the afternoon he came back to say that we should get together back in London to talk about my proposal.

The outcome was a deal that was formally announced the following spring. It was a case of the minnow swallowing the whale. Hutchinson was a group of companies with a dozen different imprints, a stable of illustrious authors, a warehouse and distribution complex in Tiptree, Essex, a property portfolio of thirty-three houses in the neighbouring village, and overseas subsidiaries in Australia and New Zealand. I had been promoted overnight from boss of an entrepreneurial start-up to CEO of a leading publishing conglomerate.

It wasn't an easy transition. The old timers at Hutchinson's London HQ didn't all take kindly to their new leader. One made a point of lounging back with his feet on the desk and a newspaper in his hands whenever I showed up in the editorial offices. Another said he would sooner climb the North Face of the Eiger than attend one of my editorial meetings.

The expanded entity of which I had taken the reins was a powerhouse of both commercial and literary publishing. My new role not only made me the lunch companion of one of the great literary drinkers, it also introduced me to a future president of the United States of America.

Kingsley Amis was awarded the Booker Prize in 1986 for his novel *The Old Devils*, published by Hutchinson, and I was, at least in theory, his editor. There were three explicit rules of engagement.

19. *The Old Devils*

For longtime admirers of the Amis of *Lucky Jim* and after,
The Old Devils is welcome evidence that the master remains
masterful... an insightful guide through the terrain where
what is said is not meant, and what is felt is not said, but
where much of life is lived.

Los Angeles Times

Kingsley Amis
THE OLD DEVILS

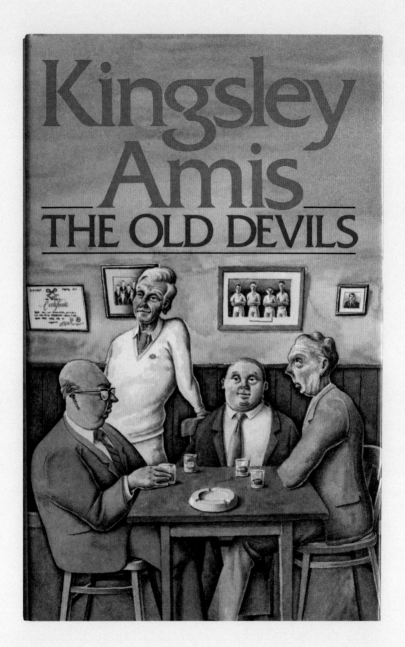

1. I was not allowed to change a single word or punctuation mark in what he wrote.
2. My primary role was to authorise a generous advance in future contracts.
3. I would have him as my guest at regular lunches at the Savoy Grill, the Ivy Restaurant or the Bombay Brasserie.

I soon found out that lunch with Kingsley Amis was, by a long way, the most dangerous of these undertakings. A separate code of conduct governed the proceedings.

The most pernicious phrase in the English language was 'Shall We Go Straight In?' Before we sat down in the dining room, there would be drinks at the bar, either a pint of ale or a martini cocktail.

Every course in the meal would be accompanied by the appropriate beverage. White burgundy for fish, vintage claret for meat, port wine for the cheese.

There would be no time limit to the duration of the meal, no covert glances at one's watch or mumbled excuses about an important meeting at the office.

At the conclusion of one of these feasts, when I was catatonic with alcohol, it was Kingsley who broke the rules by announcing that he had a four o'clock appointment for a TV interview on Channel 4. I fell into a taxi and went home to sleep it off. Kingsley hailed a cab to Channel 4 in Victoria and delivered a word-perfect account of his novel.

ooooo

The Art of the Deal, by Donald Trump, has earned a place in this memoir not for what it is but for what it wasn't. Trump claims that he didn't write it in the first place, that he'd never met the ghost writer, read the book, or approved what the ghost had written.

We published the book all the same, under the Century imprint, and invited Trump to visit the UK for the launch. He arrived at Heathrow in his private plane, accompanied by his wife Ivana and his daughter Ivanka. By the time he departed we had commissioned Ivana to write a novel. She did actually write and deliver the novel – but it was never published.

Nonetheless, Trump's book does raise an important question: what is the art of the deal in the publishing business? I've spent fifty years in search of the answers.

Here is a set of the five virtues I would recommend as the keys to a successful career in publishing:

1. *Curiosity*: an omnivorous appetite to explore any book, outline or proposal that comes one's way; fact or fiction, history, science or philosophy, science fiction, romance or detective story.
2. *Empathy*: the capacity to judge whether the writer has the skill to engage the emotions of the reader.
3. *Resilience*: the strength to live with the knowledge that the great majority of books published are destined for a short shelf life and disappointing sales.
4. *Audacity*: the boldness to put all reservations aside and go for broke when the right one hoves into sight.
5. *Optimism*: the belief that, whatever happened yesterday, tomorrow will bring new and better opportunities.

The following three books enshrine certain enduring truths about publishing, in both their titles and their content.

'Say Little, Write Nothing, Act At Once' was the succinct maxim of America's wealthiest banker, quoted in

TRUMP
THE ART OF THE DEAL

Today's hottest
tycoon **really** tells you
how he does it

DONALD TRUMP
WITH TONY SCHWARTZ

The No.1 BESTSELLER

Ron Chernow's *The House of Morgan* (2010). Once you've come to a decision, don't let anyone talk you out of it.

Feel the Fear and Do It Anyway (1987) is the title of a bestselling self-help manual by Susan Jeffers. If you want to win the auction for a really expensive book, don't be put off by the fact that anyone who wins an auction is, by definition, paying more than anyone else thinks it's worth.

Sun Tzu's *The Art of War* runs to a mere 100 pages, and was written as a strategic battlefield manual for the lords of war. It is a revered classic of Chinese philosophy written more than 2,500 years ago. Sun Tzu was a master of counter-intuitive thinking. Always go on the offensive. The attacker has everything to lose and will therefore fight all the harder to win.

ooooo

Probably the most expensive mistake of my career is that I rejected Stephen Hawking's *A Brief History of Time* (1988), which became the most successful work of cosmology of my lifetime.

I had been tracking the book for some time and had my chance to pounce on it in 1987 at the annual meeting of the American Booksellers Association in Atlanta, Georgia. By sheer coincidence, I found myself on a comfort break in the next-door urinal to Hawking's agent. He had with him a copy of the completed typescript, which he entrusted to me. I tried to read it on the plane home. *A Brief History of Time*

20. *The Art of the Deal*

Money was never a big motivation for me.
Except as a way of keeping score.
The real excitement is playing the game.

From *The Art of the Deal*

is not easy reading and I confess that I barely understood a word of it. This is an account of the Nature and Origin of the Universe in twelve not-so-easy chapters.

No matter. Back in the office we had a Science Editor who understood the mysteries of time and space and would give me the right advice. But he didn't, and we lost our chance. The rest is history.

> The physicists and mathematicians who travel the cosmic trail are the new clergy. They are not reinterpreting received wisdom or sacred texts. They are pushing out beyond the frontiers of knowledge… So, small wonder this book is selling well. We are being offered, if not a new Bible, at least the first draft of a new Genesis and Book of Revelations.
>
> Simon Jenkins on *A Brief History of Time* in *The Financial Times*

In the autumn of 1987, I flew to Moscow for a meeting with Andrei Gromyko, the President of the USSR. He had recently published a two-volume autobiography. Given that Gromyko had served both as Soviet Ambassador to the United Kingdom and as Permanent Representative of the Soviet Union to the United Nations in New York, I felt that an English-language edition would find a ready market

21. *Memories*

'Every night, whisper PEACE in your husband's ear.'

'The world may end up under a Sword of Damocles on a tightrope over the abyss.'

'The best servants of the people must whisper unpleasant truths in the master's ear.'

'An exchange of ideas takes place when you take an idea to your boss and you come back with his idea.'

Words of Russian wisdom from Andrei A. Gromyko's *Memories*

ANDREI GROMYKO
Memories

in the West. I wrote a letter to Mr Gromyko outlining our proposal. Rather to my surprise, I received an invitation to visit our prospective author in the Kremlin, as his guest. The invitation also included Hutchinson's Editorial Director, Richard Cohen, and Andrew Nurnberg, a fluent Russian speaker, who owned a literary agency in Moscow.

Andrew did the groundwork and the three of us duly landed at Sheremetyevo Airport on an Aeroflot flight. Throughout the visit we were treated as VIPs. On arrival we were ushered into a minibus decorated with artificial leopard-skin wallpaper, taken to a lounge where we were fed caviar and vodka, and whisked to our hotel in a limousine preceded by motorcycle outriders. At the hotel an affable KGB colonel introduced himself as my interpreter.

On the morrow our interpreter escorted us to the inner sanctum of the president. A tall guardsman in ceremonial uniform rode up with us in the lift. On the second floor we were greeted by the president's personal security detail: a squad of unsmiling bruisers in leather jackets. We were frisked for any concealed weapons we might be carrying.

Before us stretched a long corridor lined with gifts from previous visitors. Our KGB interpreter opened the door at the far end and introduced us to President Gromyko. My eye was drawn to the red telephone on his desk, from which a nuclear war could be launched.

We knew that Gromyko could speak excellent English, but protocol dictates that no Head of State can be addressed – or reply – in a foreign language in his own country. For an hour or more we discussed plans for Gromyko's memoirs through the medium of our bilingual KGB minder. The President concluded the meeting with an apology: he told us he was already running late for a meeting on housing problems in the Soviet Republic of Kazakhstan.

At lunch we were the guests of VAAP, the Soviet

copyright agency – a feast of Russian delicacies and toasts to Anglo-Soviet friendship. When I revealed that I had never been to the USSR before, despite the fact that my own grandmother was Russian, my hosts promptly offered to lay on a three-month tour, which would take me to all fifteen of the Soviet Socialist Republics. After lunch, the lady from VAAP wrapped her arms around me in a bear hug, kissed me on both cheeks and welcomed me on my return to the *Rodina*, the Motherland. I remember every detail of this visit because I was overwhelmed by the warmth and goodwill with which I was greeted, to the point where I felt I really *was* a child of the Motherland.

I have never published Leo Tolstoy's *War and Peace* (1869), but on the death of my father I inherited a copy of the commemorative edition published in Russia in 1906. There are three volumes, and the text is exquisitely illustrated in colour on every page.

I don't speak Russian, nor – since I was, regrettably, unable to take up the kind invitation of my Soviet hosts – do I know the country. I have lived the greater part of my life in the shadow of the Cold War and then the gangster regime of Vladimir Putin. I profoundly regret all three of these facts. There is a deeper past in which Russia was our ally in the overthrow of Napoleon and the defeat of the Third Reich. And it possesses a culture of literature, music and visual art which speaks directly to the soul.

Nowhere is this more apparent than in Tolstoy's supreme masterpiece. To my mind there is no finer novel ever written, nor a more profound testament to the values embedded in the soil of Mother Russia: the reverence for landscape, forest and farm, the rhythm of the seasons, the hunting and the drinking, the mazurka and the balalaika, the tolling of the church bells, and the quest for meaning in the quirks of birth, life, fate and death.

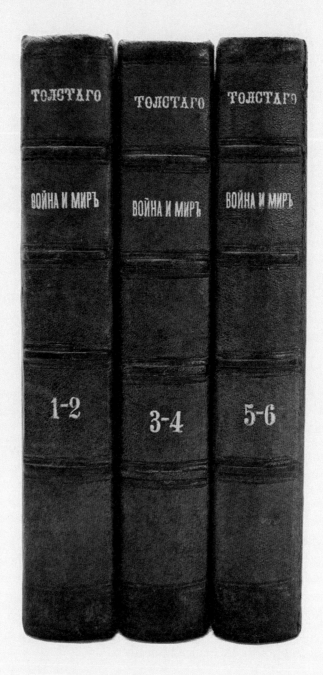

The themes of Russia's history and literature are well represented in the catalogues of a number of the publishing companies I have led: Century Hutchinson, Random House, Weidenfeld & Nicolson and Head of Zeus. Robert K. Massie's *Nicholas and Alexandra* (1967), *Peter the Great* (1980) and *Catherine the Great* (2011); Simon Sebag Montefiore's *Catherine the Great & Potemkin* (2001) and *Stalin: The Court of the Red Tsar* (2003); China Miéville's *A Spectre, Haunting* (2021); Viktor Sebestyen's *The Russian Revolution* (2023); and the novels of Sergei Lebedev on state terror, poisoned doorknobs and the superhuman courage of the late Russian opposition leader, Alexei Navalny.

Before moving on from Russia I should devote a footnote to my Russian grandmother, Anastasia Mouraviev. She was by birth neither a Russian nor a Mouraviev. But she became both when she was adopted by the imperial Russian grandee, Nikolay Mouraviev, who married her mother.

Nastia, as she was known, was famed for her beauty. At her coming-out ball, it proved necessary to hire an extra carriage to take home all the bouquets she received from her admirers. She met and married my grandfather in Rome, where Mouraviev was the Russian Ambassador and Milne Cheetham was serving as Head of Chancery at the British Embassy.

22. *War and Peace*

War and Peace is a book of essays and a book of lives in time – and not just fictional but in historical time, lives touched, shaped and maimed by events.

Excerpt from *The Novel: A Biography* (2014) by Michael Schmidt

When the First World War broke out, Nastia joined the Knights Hospitaller of St John to work as a nurse. She ministered to the wounded on the hospital ships off the beaches of Gallipoli and was awarded the Grand Cross of the Order for her services. She spent the later years of the war travelling in Egypt and the Sudan, and acted as a chaperone to HM Elizabeth the Queen Consort during a state visit to Paris in 1938. She devoted the last fifty years of her life to her cats, her ducks and her rhododendrons at Horn Hill in Buckinghamshire, where she passed away in 1976 at the age of ninety-six. Her funeral service was conducted according to the rites of the Russian Orthodox Church.

∞∞∞

In 1988 I witnessed an interesting flirtation with the celebrity-driven world of Hollywood. Rosie de Courcy had learned on the grapevine that Joan Collins was writing a novel and that Hollywood's über-agent, Irving Lazar, would be selling the rights in the UK. Joan was, at the time, the most recognisable celebrity in England thanks to her starring role as Alexis in the Denver, Colorado-based soap opera *Dynasty*. Rosie turned to London's über-agent, Ed Victor, for advice on how to snare the British rights for Century.

Irving Lazar, better known as Swifty, was said to resemble a boiled egg with his bald head but with a body pelt of frizzy black hair. When he arrived in London, Rosie rang the bell at his suite in the Ritz at 10am, bearing a bunch of roses, a bottle of expensive champagne and two glasses. Ed Victor had written the script. Swifty was a teetotaller who stayed up all night and never got out of bed until two in the afternoon. But he would be incapable of resisting a pretty face who broke all the rules.

So it came about that Century published Joan's novel, *Prime Time* (1989), and Swifty fell in love with Rosie. He offered to shower her with jewels if she would go to bed with him: it's only sex, he said.

He invited us, annually, to his Oscar Awards party in Los Angeles, where he would remind the recipients that he had made them all and that he could break them all. He introduced me to his friends as the man who would shortly be Rosie's ex-husband.

All this was pure pantomime. Swifty was a kind and generous soul who enjoyed the pretence of being an ogre. He gave me unprompted advice on the sale of Century and introduced me to his contacts among the great and the good.

12

Random House
1989–91
The deal of the century

On 7 June 1989, Publishing News announced that Random House, the leading trade publishing house in the USA, had paid £64.5m to acquire Century Hutchinson. For Century's shareholders, it was indeed the deal of the century. Seven years after a wobbly start in Soho, the other directors and I woke up one morning to discover that we were millionaires.

Odd as it may seem, this transformation brought as much sadness as it did joy. I assembled a company meeting to announce the deal and thank the Centurions for everything they had achieved. As I was speaking, I saw that some our team were actually moved to tears by the thought that we had reached the end of an era. Our brotherhood of independent pioneers had been swallowed up by the leviathan of the corporate conglomerates. The tears were infectious. My abiding memory is that of an entire roomful, including myself, of men and women united in mourning for the world we had lost.

The first issue under the new regime was the question of who would be the chief executive of Random House UK. The incumbent CEO was Simon Master, a distinguished publisher and a seasoned diplomat. He was happy to cede the role to me, and I was equally happy to cede to him. In truth, neither of us actually wanted it.

Random House UK included some of the most distinguished imprints in British publishing – Jonathan Cape, Chatto & Windus, Virago and the Bodley Head (which Random House had acquired in 1987 in its first foray into UK publishing). But the group was losing money hand over fist and the internal politics were a minefield. Chatto & Windus recorded losses greater than its annual turnover. The Bodley Head, internally known as The Oddly Dead, was on its last legs. Overheads were grossly inflated by the fact that each of the group's imprints employed separate service departments to handle production, art, publicity and the sale of rights.

Simon Master and I eventually agreed to share the role of CEO. He would be responsible for the Century Hutchinson imprints, and I would take the helm at Cape, Chatto, Virago and the Bodley Head. This proved to be a serious mistake on my part. I incurred the lifelong enmity of Carmen Callil, who resisted with tooth and claw any attempt to curb losses or meddle with the organizational structure.

The Newhouse family, who owned our parent company in New York, were remarkably tolerant of the losses we incurred in London. Their finance chief explained to me that our deficit was a drop in the ocean when compared to the billion dollar yields of their US assets. These included regional newspapers, the Condé Nast magazine empire and a near monopoly of the cable television channels in America. With their support, we were able to buy the freehold of the palatial modern office building we were based in at 20 Vauxhall Bridge Road.

The launch of Vintage Paperbacks was my most enduring contribution at Random House UK. In 1991 hardcover books and paperback reprints were still seen as two related but different kingdoms. In the realm of literary fiction and narrative non-fiction, Allen Lane's Penguin was king and Sonny Mehta's Picador was the crown prince. Our task was to persuade the captains of the literary world, from Cape and Chatto, Bodley Head and Hutchinson, to enrol under the banner of Vintage Paperbacks.

This was the remit of Frances Coady, a young editor at Cape. It wasn't easy. Jeanette Winterson came on board with *Sexing the Cherry* (1989), and Sebastian Faulks with *Birdsong* (1993). Frances had her doubts about including a set of novels by P. G. Wodehouse – pastiche, she said, but I insisted. A list was finally cobbled together and launched at a very noisy nightclub on the Thames Embankment.

All was well until the arrival of Alberto Vitale, a tough-minded accountant who was headhunted from Bantam Books to rein in the big spenders across the worldwide Random House book publishing empire. I was flown to New York by Concorde to attend his inauguration. Our first meeting was perfunctory. Our second was in New Zealand, where we fell out over his plans to flood the market with cut-price overstocks of American paperbacks. The third took place in the boardroom in Vauxhall Bridge Road, where I was summarily dismissed on the morning after Ben Okri won the Booker Prize for *The Famished Road* (1991).

I was in shock. An hour or so later I had a phone call from Ed Victor, who wanted to close the deal for a new book by Douglas Adams, the creator of the *Hitchhiker's Guide to the Galaxy* series. I thought, what the hell, and closed the deal at £1.1m. It was the first and last time that I bought a book for a company that no longer employed me.

When I look back on my time at the helm of Random House, there are three other authors and projects that I remember with lasting affection.

Roald Dahl's *The Vicar of Nibbleswicke* is the shortest of the stories written by the most successful children's author of my lifetime. In twenty-four pages it describes the plight of a dyslexic vicar who says everything back to front. Dahl wrote the story at the request of a charity, the Dyslexia Institute, shortly before he died in 1990.

When I took the helm at Random House, Dahl was at the height of his fame. His stories for children had sold more than 300 million copies around the world, and been adapted as record-breaking productions for film, theatre and television.

He was also remembered for his distinguished wartime service as a spy, a diplomat and a fighter ace. In 1986 he turned down the offer of an OBE in the Queen's Birthday Honours list on the grounds that he wanted his wife to be addressed as Lady Dahl, for which he would have required a Knighthood and not an OBE.

23. *The Vicar of Nibbleswicke*

It was the local doctor who guessed what was wrong. 'What you've got is a very rare disease called Back-to-Front Dyslexia… Fortunately there is a simple cure.

You must walk backwards while you are speaking, then these back-to-front words will come out frontwards or the right way round. It's common sense.'

From *The Vicar of Nibbleswicke*

ROALD DAHL | THE VICAR OF NIBBLESWICKE

ROALD DAHL

THE VICAR OF
NIBBLESWICKE

ILLUSTRATED BY
QUENTIN BLAKE

Not long before he died in November 1990, I was summoned to see the great man at his Buckinghamshire home in Great Missenden. He said he wanted to meet the big bad wolf now in charge of Random House and the Jonathan Cape imprint. I was given a guided tour of the estate and the gypsy caravan in which he wrote his stories, by hand, on a rigid timetable of four hours per diem.

After he died I bought the manuscript of *The Vicar of Nibbleswicke* and the original illustrations by Quentin Blake from the Dyslexia Foundation at a public auction. The twenty-four illustrations line a corridor in my country retreat.

I was alarmed to hear recently that the author of such classics as *Charlie and The Chocolate Factory*, *Matilda* and *The BFG*, *Fantastic Mr Fox* and *The Minpins* had come under fire from sensitivity readers at Puffin Books. Publishing and censorship are uneasy bedfellows, and there is relief to be found in the latest news that both versions, the author's original and the sanitised ones, are to be made available in the Puffin catalogue.

The Mysterious Press is the creation of Otto Penzler, a German-born American who knows more about crime fiction than anyone else on earth. He founded The Mysterious Press in 1975. He has collected a fabulous library of

24. *Otto Penzler's Mysterious Press Bookshop*

The King of American Crime Fiction,
The Owner of the Mysterious Bookshop,
The Founder of The Mysterious Press

first editions, published a stellar cast of mystery writers, and edited a vast array of anthologies. He indulges his passions for Italian cooking, American baseball and beautiful women.

He and I first met in New York in 1985 in his magnificent Art Deco HQ on 55th Street, where he held court and dispensed vintage champagne. In 1991 we met again in London to talk about the UK launch of his imprint in partnership with Random House. That plan was torpedoed by my uncomfortable breakfast with Alberto Vitale.

Nonetheless, we stayed in close touch. Over the next thirty years Otto and I worked together to publish a stellar collection of the great and the good in American crime fiction: Michael Connelly's Hieronymus ('Harry') Bosch and his Lincoln Lawyer series, Robert Crais and James Lee Burke, George Pelecanos and Robert Bloch, Harlan Coben and Thomas H. Cook.

Ben Okri's *The Famished Road* was awarded the Booker Prize in 1991. He and I met in the limousine that took us and his publisher, Tom Maschler (head of Jonathan Cape), to the award ceremony at the City of London's Guildhall. I was at first a little bit intimidated by this prodigy who had stormed the citadel of Britain's literary establishment with a 500-page dream fantasy of Nigerian myth and magic. To describe Ben as an author is in itself an understatement.

25. *The Famished Road*

In the beginning there was a river. The river became a road and the road branched out to the whole world. And because the road was once a river it was always hungry.

Opening paragraph

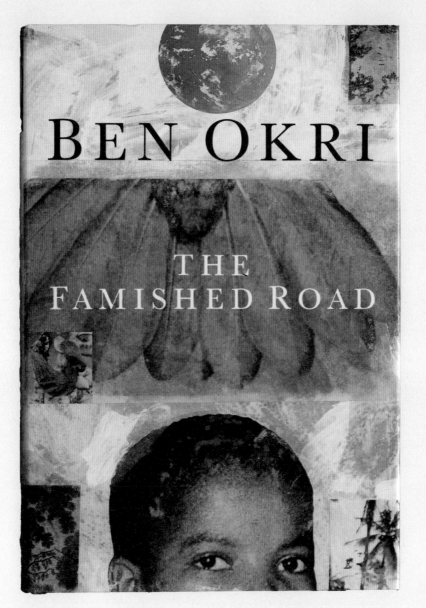

BEN OKRI

THE
FAMISHED ROAD

He is a master artist who has devoted himself to all nine of the classical muses.

Ben has never wavered in his friendship towards me or his loyalty. Head of Zeus is now the primary publisher of Ben's new novels, children's stories, plays and poetry.

My own favourite among his many books has to be *Every Leaf A Hallelujah* (2021), an ecological plea on behalf of the world's forests. I invented the storyline and acted it out in front of Ben and the astonished publishing team assembled in the Head of Zeus boardroom. Ben has since adapted the story for performance as a musical. In exchange, I have been giving his daughter Mirabella lessons in driving my green garden buggy, a privilege customarily reserved for my grandchildren.

THE BOOKSELLER 29 MAY 1992   £1·50

BOOKSELLER

THE ORGAN OF THE BOOK TRADE

J.M.Dent
1888

Weidenfeld & Nicolson
1948

Orion Books
1992

The Orion Publishing Group

13

The Orion Publishing Group
1991–2003
A Big Bang and a sad whimper

In the days following my expulsion from Random House,
one of the first people to get in touch was George
Weidenfeld, chairman and proprietor of Weidenfeld &
Nicolson. He and I had first met in the early years of my
career, when I was commissioned to write *The Life and
Times of Richard III* (1972).

George's company had fallen on hard times. He no
longer enjoyed the support of his erstwhile patron, Anne
Getty, and had moved his offices from the West End of
London to the outskirts of Clapham. George asked me
whether I would be interested in taking the helm at W&N.
I had already taken steps to start a new company under the
name of Orion Books, but he was keen to see whether we
could run both projects in harness.

And so, in 1991, the Orion Publishing Group was born
(the troublesome bank of the same name having ceased to
exist). We raised money from a venture capital partnership
named Phoenix, and moved into a smart new office building,

fortuitously named Orion House, in St Martin's Lane, and launched the company in 1992. Over the next decade we published a remarkable list in all categories, from history and science to crime, thrillers, science fiction, literary classics and children's books.

George Weidenfeld held an honorary position as chairman of W&N. His role, as he described it himself, was to act as the impresario who would introduce me to the great and the good at lavish dinner parties under the gaze of the Francis Bacon portrait of a cardinal on the wall of his Chelsea dining room. In exchange he received an eye-watering expense account of £80,000 per annum.

It was at one of these dinners that I first met Krzysztof Michalski, a Polish philosopher who felt he had come of age only when he could read Kant's *Critique of Pure Reason* (1781) in the original German. He became and remained a close friend until his untimely death in February 2013. We called him K for short.

In 1982 Krzysztof founded the Institut für die Wissenschaften vom Menschen/Institute for Human Sciences (IWM) in Vienna. His purpose was to provide a neutral meeting place between East and West. It was a visionary initiative that put him at the heart of European politics for the next thirty years. IWM seminars were regularly attended by ministers and heads of state from both sides of the Iron Curtain.

Krzysztof was also a devout Catholic. As a student at Warsaw University, he had been tutored by Karol Józef Wojtyła, the cleric who was elected as Pope John Paul II in 1978. He was invited by his mentor to host an annual seminar at the Pope's summer retreat in Castel Gandolfo. It was also suggested that he should draft the Pope's spiritual autobiography.

George Weidenfeld rose like a hungry shark to the challenge of publishing this book. K was invited to dine in Chelsea, and I was invited to attend a seminar at the IWM in Vienna. This was where I met Krzysztof's partner, Cornelia Klinger.

The Viennese seminar was but the first of the junkets I attended as a guest of the IWM or the Bertelsmann Foundation. I became an honorary member of an elite corps of philosophers drawn from the world's leading universities. The climax was a visit to the Vatican and an introduction to the Pope. One by one we advanced in line to kneel at his feet, where we received his blessing and a medal to commemorate the event. Later we were invited to dinners and receptions in the palaces of the Italian and Roman aristocracy: Pallavicini, Colonna, Orsini, Frescobaldi, Schwarzenberg. I was mildly disappointed not to find a Borgia amongst them, but I was placed one evening next to a lady by the name of Habsburg. I asked how many others of her line would have stood between her and the imperial crown if the Dual Monarchy had survived the Great War. None, she replied.

Krzysztof did eventually complete John Paul's autobiography, but the Pope died in 2005 before it had been vetted by his secretary and approved for publication.

The only book Krzysztof wrote that is available in an English translation (by Benjamin Paloff) is *The Flame of Eternity* (2011), a meditation on Nietzsche's concept of eternity, which he wrote in my Cotswold garden. Every word of every sentence had to be polished until it gleamed like a star in the sky.

When he learned that he was suffering from a fatal cancer, he insisted that his illness must remain a secret. Instead he invited us to join him and his partner on a farewell autumn weekend at a farmhouse bed and breakfast

IAN RANKIN

Strip Jack

AN INSPECTOR REBUS NOVEL

hotel in Upper Austria. Not a word was spoken about the cancer. We were due to meet again in Vienna in the New Year, but he died on 11 February 2013 before we got there.

We have kept in touch with Cornelia Klinger, who succeeded him as Rector at the IWM. We exchange video calls at Christmas and, when she visits us in summer, we lay flowers at the foot of the beech tree he planted in our woods.

ooooo

Strip Jack by Ian Rankin marked the debut of his ingenious sleuth, Detective Inspector Rebus, and the start of an unmatched career, which has given his publishers twenty-two national bestsellers. He and I would meet annually for a gourmet lunch at Edinburgh's No 1 Princes Street. The rules of engagement were that I would order an unlimited supply of Premier Cru claret, and the maître d' would shovel me into a taxi at 3.30pm to catch the teatime flight back to London.

Michael Connelly's *The Poet* (1996) was not his first novel, nor does it feature his most famous protagonist, the Los Angeles Police Department's Hieronymus Bosch, whose investigations have decorated bestseller lists on both sides of the Atlantic for the past thirty years. The Poet of the title is a professional hit man. The novel is written in the form of a first-person memoir. I will always remember its chilling opening line: 'Death is my beat. I make my living from it.'

26. *Strip Jack*

In 2005 Rankin became the tenth bestselling writer in Britain, accounting for 10 percent of all crime fiction sold.

Guardian

I first met Michael Connelly when he came to the UK for an author tour. He was whisked straight from Heathrow to my country retreat and subjected to a very liquid Sunday lunch. In the afternoon I invited him to choose a tree, which would bear his name in commemoration of his visit. He chose a hundred-year-old willow tree, which had seen better days and was clearly on the point of collapse. He said that it resembled his own state of health after the ordeal of a Sunday lunch with Anthony Cheetham. The willow has since collapsed but new growth has sprouted from the fallen trunk, and it is known to this day as the Connelly Tree.

A Suitable Boy (1993) by Vikram Seth is a masterpiece of twentieth-century literary fiction in 1,398 pages. It first came to my attention when Nicholas Pearson, then a junior editor at Weidenfeld, rang me at home on a Sunday while I was mowing the lawn. He was, quite literally, in tears after reading Vikram's novel and felt I should know about it at once.

I invited Vikram's agent to a meeting and secured the rights for a pre-emptive advance of £250,000. It was a lot of money in those days. Vikram didn't win the Booker Prize, as we had hoped, but the sales were extraordinary, and *A Suitable Boy* dominated the bestseller lists. We published several editions, including a boxed set in three volumes.

27. *The Poet*

Death is my beat. I make my living from it. I forge my professional relationship on it. I treat it with the passion and precision of an undertaker – somber and sympathetic about it when I'm with the bereaved, a skilled craftsman with it when I'm alone. I've always thought the secret to dealing with death was to keep it at arm's length. That's the rule. Don't let it breathe in your face.

Opening words

POET

HE KILLS. WITHOUT RHYME OR REASON

MICHAEL CONNELLY

A
SUITABLE
BOY

VIKRAM SETH

Nothing that Vikram has written since *A Suitable Boy* has come near to matching the grandeur, the colours or the genius of his masterpiece. His plans to write a sequel entitled *A Suitable Girl* have been announced but not fulfilled.

A postscript on the 1993 Booker Prize: Lord Gowrie, the chair of the judges, wrote a rather silly article in the *Guardian* explaining why the prize had not been awarded, as expected, to Vikram.

When asked for my reaction, I replied that Gowrie (Eton and Balliol) was a wanker. The reporter asked if he could quote me. By all means, I said, provided that the word 'wanker' was spelled out in full without the asterisks conventionally used to mask vulgar expressions. The next morning my quote duly appeared – unasterisked – on the front page of the *Guardian*. As far as I know it's the only time my name or the word 'wanker' have both appeared on the front page of a national newspaper.

The Six Wives of Henry VIII by Antonia Fraser was first published by Weidenfeld & Nicolson in 1971. Her biography of Mary, Queen of Scots, was the book that launched her career, but *The Six Wives* was her most successful book ever. In 1993, we persuaded her that it would be a good idea to republish the hardcover at the bargain price of £10. It worked, and she referred to this edition ever after as 'El Cheapo'.

28. *A Suitable Boy*

A Suitable Boy is not only one of the longest novels in English: it may also prove to be the most fecund as well as the most prodigious work of the latter half of the twentieth century. I have little doubt that Vikram is already the best writer of his generation.

Daniel Johnson, *The Times*

Antonia and her extended family have been outstanding friends and supporters throughout my life as a publisher, ever since I contributed a biography of Richard III to her series on the Kings and Queens of England.

Before he wrote about trees, Antonia's brother, Thomas, was already recognised as a leading historian, author of *The Boer War* (1979) and *The Scramble for Africa* (1991). I visited him at his family home, Tullynally Castle, in County Westmeath, a monstrous Gothic pile with so many rooms, floors and turrets that first-time guests need a guide to locate their allotted quarters. The broad acres of the surrounding estate were home to the forest he had planted.

Thomas was also an accomplished photographer. Equipped with a bulky box camera and a time-lapse device, he would focus the lens on a favourite tree and scurry to appear in the foreground of the tree when the image was taken.

I was immediately smitten with the idea of publishing his photographs in a large-format illustrated book. Thomas hated the title, which I had stolen from the Armenian mystic G. I. Gurdjieff's *Meetings with Remarkable Men* (1960). But

29. *The Six Wives of Henry VIII*

Thank goodness this is not one more book about the old monster, but about the women in his life and from their point of view.

A. L. Rowse, *Evening Standard*

She lays bare the battle of the sexes among the early Tudor ruling classes in a way that has never been done before.

Paul Johnson, *Sunday Telegraph*

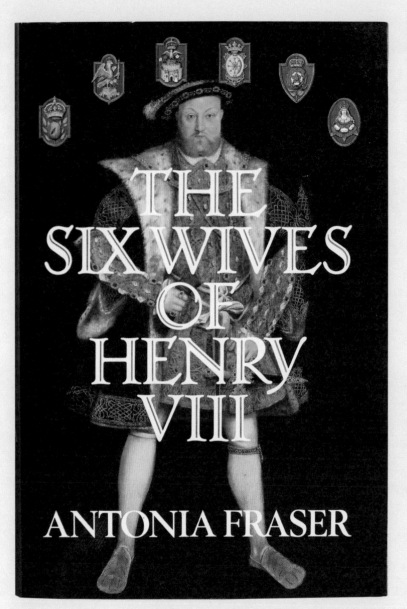

THE
SIX WIVES
OF
HENRY
VIII

ANTONIA FRASER

MEETINGS WITH REMARKABLE TREES

THOMAS PAKENHAM

Lady Antonia disagreed and persuaded him that my title was an act of homage rather than theft.

The book sold more than 200,000 copies in its original format and remains in print to this day. It also marked the beginning of my own love affair with trees.

Thirty years ago I bought 75 acres of farmland in the Cotswolds and planted 30,000 trees. They were whips, no more than three foot high. Today they reach fifty feet into the sky. They reinvent themselves in each season of the year: the spartan architecture of bare branches and columns of light in winter, bursts of blossom in the spring, a palette of a thousand shades of green in high summer, red and gold leaves in the autumn. Oak, ash, hornbeam, willow, may, field maple, bird cherry and chestnut.

A modest arboretum features some oddities that caught my fancy: the weeping blue cedar from the High Atlas, swamp cypress from the Florida Everglades, snakebark maples and giant bamboo from Japan, mountain eucalyptus from New South Wales, giant sequoias from the American North West, and the dawn redwood, *Metasequoia glyptostroboides*, discovered in China's Hu'nan province in 1939, some 60 million years after it was supposed to have become extinct.

I am lost in awe at this class of beings which even now outnumbers humanity by a thousand to one.

30. *Meetings with Remarkable Trees*

Trees arrived on earth millions of years before we did. And even today they outnumber us by more than a thousand to one.

The Birth of the Modern (1991) by Paul Johnson is a thesis of more than a thousand pages on the transformation that took place across the world in the critical years between 1815 and 1830. He explores in astonishing detail every facet of politics and economics, science and technology, art and literature. *The Birth of the Modern* is the masterwork of a historian who published more than fifty books and innumerable articles during his lifetime.

When I arrived at Weidenfeld & Nicolson, Paul adopted the role of overseer to ensure that I was fit to be the CEO of the company that George Weidenfeld had founded in 1949.

Nineteen ninety-three was the annus mirabilis for the Orion Group. Five of our authors dominated the upper reaches of *The Sunday Times* bestseller list. I have already written above about *A Suitable Boy* by Vikram Seth, who became known as the Indian Tolstoy. We also published *Highgrove: Portrait of an Estate* (1993) by HRH The Prince of Wales and Charles Clover, in a joint venture with Ian and Marjorie Chapman. Antonia Fraser bounded back into the bestsellers with the £10 hardback of *The Six Wives of Henry VIII*. While *Diana v. Charles* (1993), an album of photographs compiled by James Whitaker for the *Daily Mail*, sold upwards of a million copies. And the indiscreet but compulsive *Diaries* (1993) of Alan Clark leapt straight into the list at number one.

31. *The Birth of the Modern*

… what makes this elephantine work an unexpected pleasure is… the author's sheer enthusiasm for making the tiniest fragments of recorded history burst with light and color.

Jeffrey Scheuer, *Los Angeles Times*

PAUL JOHNSON

THE BIRTH OF THE MODERN

-WORLD SOCIETY 1815-1830-

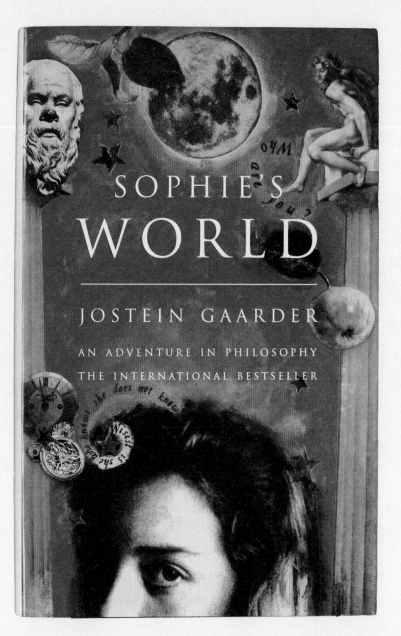

SOPHIE'S
WORLD

JOSTEIN GAARDER

AN ADVENTURE IN PHILOSOPHY
THE INTERNATIONAL BESTSELLER

Jostein Gaarder was a Norwegian schoolmaster. He was deeply upset when philosophy was removed from the school curriculum in his country. *Sophie's World* (1995) is the book he wrote in protest. It is written not as a treatise but as a novel for young adults: playful, charming, emotive and mysterious, all at once.

In her mailbox Sophie finds a series of clues to a treasure hunt, which she has to solve in order to unravel for herself the key concepts of humankind and Western philosophy. *Sofies Verden* proved to be a huge success when it was first published in Norway in 1991.

I had to pay an uncomfortably large advance for UK and Commonwealth rights, which were fiercely contested by Tom Maschler at Jonathan Cape. His reputation as a genius of publishing was such that it actually encouraged me to come up with the money to win the auction.

Sophie's World topped the bestseller lists and sold more than a million copies. My fifteen-year-old daughter, Emma, then a pupil at Cheltenham Ladies College, played a significant part in the marketing campaign when she presented the book at her school assembly.

The Science Masters (1995) is a series masterminded by John Brockman, the steely-eyed American literary agent and entrepreneur who ushered the publishing industry into the digital age. He was not a man to suffer fools gladly. Our first

32. *Sophie's World*

Sophie's World is set to become a unique popular classic: a wonderfully engaging mystery story that also forms a completely accessible and lucid introduction to philosophy and philosophers.

The Times

meeting took place over breakfast at the Dorchester Hotel in Park Lane. I outlined to him the idea of commissioning the leading scientists of the day to report from the front lines on the issues and problems they were working on at the time. He heard me out, made no further comment and said he would get back to me. The meeting was over in less than ten minutes. I assumed that he'd closed me down as quickly as he could because he was not remotely interested in my proposal.

Two days later he phoned me from Japan to tell me that he had enlisted sixteen of the world's leading scientists to contribute to a series entitled *The Science Masters*. The authors that Brockman recruited were a roll-call of the great and the good in the world of science. They included Richard Dawkins, Jared Diamond, Richard Leakey, Daniel Dennett, Lee Smolin, Steven Pinker, Susan Greenfield and Martin Rees. The series eventually ran to twenty-four titles on subjects ranging from sex to mathematics, cosmology to genetics, the origins of mankind to the behaviour of horses.

The Science Masters was launched at the Cheltenham Literary Festival in October 1995 at a press conference chaired by Douglas Adams, author of the hugely popular *Hitchhiker's Guide to the Galaxy*. I got used to John Brockman's staccato way of doing business and over the years we became good friends. I believe we even agreed that his son Max should marry my daughter Rebecca. That didn't happen.

33. *The Science Masters*

Sixteen world-class scientists define the boundaries of modern science, and the next steps on the road to discovery.

THE
HUMAN
BRAIN

A GUIDED TOUR

SUSAN
GREENFIELD

CHRONICLES OF ANCIENT DARKNESS

WOLF
BROTHER

MICHELLE PAVER

Wolf Brother (2004) is the first of twelve adventures in *The Chronicles of Ancient Darkness* by Michelle Paver. In this sequence, Michelle has created a time machine that takes us back to the Stone Age.

We see the world through the eyes of an orphan named Torak and the nose of his Wolf Brother. Together, the boy and the wolf must unite the clans and overcome the supernatural powers of a malignant entity bent on the destruction of humankind. It is a thrilling journey, packed with suspense and backed by the author's painstaking research into the prehistoric past.

The series was acquired by our children's publisher, Fiona Kennedy, who received an offer of $1m from HarperCollins for the US rights. She turned it down. I was horrified, but she was right. The final price was $1.55m.

Fiona has a happy knack of publishing beautifully illustrated books by prize-winning authors. She is now publisher of Zephyr, the children's imprint at Head of Zeus.

ooooo

The middle years of the 1990s saw the beginning of a controversy that split the book community down the middle and heralded a profound change in the fortunes of the publishing industry.

In August 1994 the Office of Fair Trading (OFT) called for a review of the Net Book Agreement (NBA). The NBA

34. *Wolf Brother*

Wolf Brother is the kind of story you dream of reading and all too rarely find. The descriptions of an ancient world are wonderful. The vivid prose leaps off the page.

The Times

stipulated that publishers had the legal right to determine the retail prices of their goods and booksellers were bound to maintain them.

The issues at stake were fiercely debated. Abolitionists argued that lower prices would see a significant increase in sales. Defenders of Retail Price Maintenance (RPM) feared that independent booksellers would be put out of business by supermarket chains and newsagents.

As a council member of the Publishers Association, I had a ringside seat at the debate. I voted at first with the abolitionists, led by Richard Charkin, but changed sides when I saw just how apprehensive the Booksellers Association were about the consequences. Nonetheless, the OFT sided with abolition and retail price maintenance was outlawed in March 1997.

It hurts to record how much the bookselling community has shrunk in the years that followed. At the time of abolition, the UK market was served by four national chain booksellers. At Ottokar's the customer was invited to sink into a comfortable armchair with a café latte while selecting their next purchase. Specialist library suppliers in Lancashire and the Midlands provided a career path for new fiction writers by ordering sheets from publishers and binding them up with needle and thread for sale to public libraries. Bookwise was a nationwide wholesale business that distributed paperbacks to confectioners, tobacconists and newsagents.

And more important than any of these was Book Club Associates (BCA), a mail-order business licensed to sell books at a discount to members of their clubs. There were seventeen of these clubs, catering to specialist interests from Military and Aviation to Ancient and Medieval, Science Fiction and Fantasy to Mystery and Thrillers. The greatest prize was a Main Selection across all their clubs, which could yield an order of 100,000 copies.

BCA's German owners, Bertelsmann AG, sold the business in 2011. Within a year it was bankrupt and ceased to exist. It was a sad ending for the business founded in 1950 by Reinhard Mohn, a German prisoner-of-war who dreamed up the idea in a Scottish internment camp.

The**Bookseller**

10 October 2003/£4.40

www.theBookseller.com

UNAUTHORISED RETURNS

A Gallic stabbing over the full English

ILLUSTRATION BY IAN POLLOCK

O! What a fall there was, my countrymen . . . By one of those coincidences that happen only in real life, the Friends of Cheetham were in the middle of their conference in Eastbourne when the news broke. Once a year we gather in some genteel spa or other to relive old glories and generally exchange reminiscences of England's Greatest Living Bookman.

As it happened I was making the opening remarks of my ground-breaking paper, "The Cheethams: A Publishing Dynasty", when one of our younger members burst into the room waving his mobile phone and babbling incoherently. Suppressing my irritation (in the spirit of the Master, we are nothing if not amiable), I asked what was the matter.

Seizing his moment in the spotlight, young Justin cleared his throat. "Anthony. Cheetham. Has. Been. Fired," he intoned. "By. The. French." I allowed the subsequent hubbub to go on for a minute or two before I took control. "Gentlemen (and Lady), I think this calls for a drink," I said, and led them to the bar.

Some hours later and somewhat the worse for wear, I decided that there was no point in continuing the conference, especially since our Guest of Honour, Dallas Manderson, who was due to regale us with a few remarks after dinner, would presumably have pressing business elsewhere. So we went our separate ways.

What was it about Our Hero that made American or French gentlemen (so-called) feel they could come over here, invite him to breakfast and then stab him in the back? It was perhaps unwise of him to describe Jean-Louis Lisimachio, who resigned after disagreements with his superiors to be replaced by Arnaud Nourry, as "a good egg", whether fried, poached or lightly boiled. Even more unwise, perhaps, to stand up at a sales conference and remind his bosses that his retirement date was looming and that it was up to his employer whether he went or not. Perhaps literal-minded Frenchmen thought to themselves, well, if it's up to us, let's get rid of him, invite him

to a *petit déjeuner*. Gallic shrug. I hope at least Anthony got a decent full English out of it.

Public statements were pretty anodyne as usual: "Time for a change" and all that. And after what we will come to think of as the Dave Pelzer years too. Wasn't that change enough? Peter Roche, who has been at our man's side from the beginning, issued a curious statement that was almost Pinteresque (or do I mean Beckettian?) in its bleakness: "There was no row, no nothing."

No nothing. Here is our Greatest Living Englishman forced out on his ear by perfidious Gauls—over an Englishman's favourite meal, what's more—and that's nothing? But as more details came out, talk of Beckett (or do I mean Pinter?) came to seem eerily apposite, as the drama began to take on the aspects of a tragedy that was positively Shakespearian. "There's such divinity doth hedge a king/That treason can but peep to what it would," as Claudius put it, getting it slightly wrong as usual.

Skateboarder's Weekly dutifully came up with a conspiracy theory, involving dirty work at the *carrefour*. Apparently, various senior colleagues of Cheetham had taken to slipping over to Paris to complain to the Dauphin about their distinguished colleague's . . . what? Erratic behaviour? Heavy-handed management? The Organ, descending regrettably into tittle-tattle, quoted a "former colleague" as describing him as "impatient and difficult". Well, of course! Whenever geniuses, especially publishing geniuses, find themselves surrounded by lesser mortals, they become impatient and

difficult! Think of Peter Mayer! Tom Maschler! André Deutsch! Tom Rosenthal! Peter Straus!

Whatever they were, his so-called failings, these unnamed "senior colleagues" (there are only so many of them) must have been blessing the advent of Eurostar, but a short stroll over the river from Orion House. So much handier for "working at home" than Heathrow.

No doubt the slow drip of complaint from these midgets had the desired effect, hence the breakfast of the long knives, which had been preceded by plenty of *déjeuners des poignards longs*, I dare say. Five-course blowouts at La Tour d'Argent, followed by a little light *trahison* with the *digestif*, then a taxi back over the river to the Gare du Nord. What could be more pleasant?

Still, it's all over now, and no real Cheetham admirer would want him to labour away at his age somewhere he isn't wanted. One wishes Messrs Roche, Edwards, Manderson and de Cacqueray—not forgetting Ms Lamb, of course—luck in following in the footsteps of what *The Bookseller* described as "the last of his kind". My advice to them is to scrutinise the expenses claims of their colleagues very carefully, or they too will find themselves saying, "Et tu, senior colleague?" before long.

As for EGLB himself, he declares himself not finished and hints at new glories to come. There was a picture of him cavorting with dinosaurs in last week's *Skateboarder's Weekly*. If this is a clue, it's a rather ambiguous one.

WILLIAM BOOT

boot@bookseller.co.uk

14

The French Connection
2003

Hachette traverse la Manche

The Orion years were the most interesting and adventurous years of my career. But I overplayed my hand. We went too far and too fast. We published too many books across too many different imprints, missed our budget forecasts and ran out of cash.

Looking back at the catalogues of the Orion Publishing Group for 1998 and 1999, I am simply bemused by the range of the imprints we owned and the number of authors we published. Our imprints included J. M. Dent, Everyman Classics, Millennium Science Fiction, Phoenix paperbacks, and lists devoted to law, business and popular dogs.

We did all we could to put our house in order, sold our law books and abandoned the Everyman Classics. But it was not enough. In 1999 the Orion Group would record losses of £4m on sales of £50m. Phoenix Capital Partners, our backers in the acquisition of Weidenfeld & Nicolson, decided to put Orion on the block and sell the business to the highest bidder. We were in no position to argue.

In the summer of 1998 I made sales pitches and presentations in London, Paris, New York and Washington. It was in Paris that we found the new owner of the Orion Publishing Group. The winning bid came from Hachette Livre, the leading publishing group in France. *Hachette traverse la Manche* was a headline in *Le Monde* on the morning after the deal was announced on 3 August 1998.

Our new chief was Jean-Louis Lisimachio, a man of many parts. I remember him as modest, punctilious and supportive. He would travel by train every month to Waterloo Station wearing a dark suit and pushing an overnight wheelie bag. He treated us with courtesy and respect, but no detail in our monthly accounts ever escaped his eye. He was a self-made scholar from a working-class background in Provence who had won top honours at the École Polytechnique in Paris.

Jean-Louis's mission was to establish a secure and lasting role for Hachette as a market leader in English-language publishing, both in Britain and in the USA. At his behest, we moved quickly to buy the reference book publisher Cassell & Co. in December 1998.

To our lasting regret, Jean-Louis would be ousted from his role as my chairman as a result of the power struggle within Hachette's owners, the Lagardère Group, in May 2003.

The acquisition of Cassell brought Orion a high-quality reference list, an immense backlist of popular military titles, and one of the most resonant brand names in twentieth-century British publishing – Victor Gollancz Ltd. The firm had a venerable past as the publisher of many of the most important writers of the twentieth century, from George Orwell and Daphne du Maurier to Kingsley Amis and John le Carré. But its glory days were in the past: most of the major authors had departed, and those who remained were licensed out in paperback to our competitors. I took the unpopular decision to focus instead on its science fiction and fantasy list, which had remained a strong commercial presence in the UK book trade since the 1960s.

The man who transformed Victor Gollancz Science Fiction into Britain's market leader was Malcolm Edwards, managing director of Orion Books and a former publishing director of Gollancz in its pre-Cassell days. Malcolm accepted the challenge of building the perfect backlist, an A to Z of science fiction from Asimov to Zelazny. A few years later, when I lost my job at Orion, Malcolm told me that he had learned a great deal from my example. The truth is that I learned a great deal more from him than he ever did from me.

Light by M. John Harrison (2002) is my all-time favourite science-fiction novel. It hasn't sold nearly as many copies as Frank Herbert's *Dune* or Liu Cixin's *The Three-Body Problem*, but it leaves an indelible mark on the emotions as well as the mind.

At the heart of the story is The Shrander, an alien of a dying species that has failed the test of learning how to navigate the far reaches of space-time and survive the unpredictable terrors of a quantum universe. The Shrander reveals that it has dedicated its life to the breeding of a human bloodline that can meet the challenge of the stars in the Kefahuchi Tract, 'a singularity without an event horizon'.

The emotional impact of the story resides in the loneliness and pathos of this extraterrestrial visitor, the last of its kind, who has dedicated a lifespan measured in millions of years to the creation of a species that will succeed where its own has failed.

As a testament to my regard for Harrison's masterpiece, I keep in my library the author's original typescript, the uncorrected book proof, the advance reading copy sent out

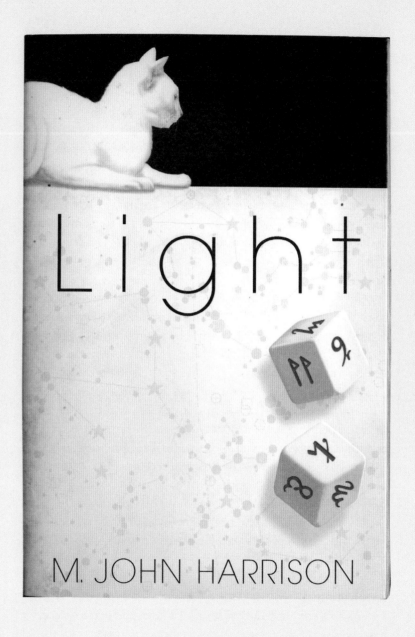

Light

M. JOHN HARRISON

to bookstores, and the hardcover of the Gollancz edition from 2002.

ooooo

As part of the expanded Orion, Cassell & Co. became home to a family of commercially successful illustrated books, among them *The Beatles Anthology*. Published by Cassell in 2000, this is the closest we shall ever see to an autobiography of the Fab Four, a monumental illustrated book with a detailed chronology and texts of all of their lyrics, doodles and notes to one another.

The man who acquired this book was John Mitchinson, whom I had recruited as Cassell's Deputy Publisher. John is a mercurial and talented entrepreneur who went on to edit the QI – Quite Interesting – anthologies for Faber and to found Unbound, the first crowd-funded publishing venture.

At the same time, we launched an outstanding programme of reference books. The star title is *Cassell's Chronology of World History: Dates, Events and Ideas That Made History* (2005), by Hywel Williams. This 800-page tome has no place to rest on my bookshelves: it is permanently on duty at my side as a fact check on dates in political and military history, in science, technology and the arts. The entries take us from the first appearance of *Homo sapiens*

35. *Light*

John Harrison proves that science fiction can be literature of the very greatest kind. *Light* puts most modern fiction to shame. It's a magnificent book.

China Miéville

in Africa 135,000 years ago to 2004 in the Christian Era. It has been my invaluable guide and companion for the past twenty years. I revere the industry and ingenuity of an author who has amassed such a wealth of information in a single volume.

ooooo

In 2003, it was my turn to be dismissed by Jean-Louis Lisimachio's successor, Arnaud Nourry, over breakfast in a Covent Garden hotel. Nourry was a corporate thug who cited a legal loophole in my service contract in order to devalue the final payment due to me on the sale of my Orion shares.

An unfortunate outcome of my dismissal was the end of my thirty-year association with our finance director, Peter Roche. At Futura, Century, Hutchinson, Random House and Orion, Peter had steered us through the rocks of venture capital, budget shortfalls and cash crises. He and I had shared many of the best moments in my career both at home and abroad.

ooooo

A final word on the legacy of my years with the Orion Publishing Group.

The Phoenix Giants form a cache of 440 large-format paperbacks we assembled as a showcase for the treasures on our backlist. It is a non-fiction list ranging from astronomy to zoology. I like to imagine that, collectively, they represent a useful summary of human history and achievement.

The Publishing Director of Phoenix Giants was Bing Taylor, formerly head book buyer at W. H. Smith and CEO of Book Club Associates. He was guided in his turn by the genius of Simon Schama. The list was discontinued soon after I left Orion. I believe that the only complete set of

Phoenix Giants is the one I keep in my study at home. There is not room here for a list of all 440 titles. But if I was compelled to choose just two books for a one-way trip to a desert island in the South Pacific, I would leave aside the well-known classics and plump instead for *Goethe* by Richard Friedenthal and *Vestal Fire* by Stephen J. Pyne.

The first English edition of *Goethe: His Life and Times* was published in 1963. The author not only portrays Goethe as a giant of world literature, but also provides 'a picture of the man in his completeness… at times vulgar, ribald, a dandy, carouser, politician, social lion and flirt'. The book runs to 560 rich and rewarding pages.

Stephen J. Pyne is a distinguished professor, explorer and environmental historian. His *Vestal Fire* (1997) is a complete history of fire and its role in shaping landscapes, forests and farming over three millennia. Pyne is also the author of *The Ice* (2003), a remarkable study of Antarctica, described by Simon Schama as 'a masterpiece… one of the greatest things ever written on the cultural history of the Earth'.

15

Quercus Publishing
2004–09

Snatching defeat from the jaws of victory

In 2004 I joined Mark Smith and Wayne Davies as Executive Chairman of a new company named after my favourite tree. There were two strands to the programme. Wayne was the man in charge of the first, which specialised in packaging illustrated reference books for sale to chain booksellers in the USA. We called it Smart Reference publishing. Mark was the managing director. My role was to create a trade list of fiction and non-fiction.

Our first and greatest success in the smart reference list was *Speeches That Changed the World* (2005). It proved to be the foundation stone of the company's fortunes and sold more than a million copies around the world. *Speeches That Changed the World* was the model for the flotilla of smart reference books we launched annually.

The Broken Shore is a rare example of a book that is both a genre crime thriller and a masterwork of literary fiction. The *Melbourne Age* declared that 'Temple puts into words some aspect of experience that makes you catch your breath it's so perfectly realised'.

On the surface this is the story of a murder investigation conducted by a detective named Joe Cashin, who has quit Melbourne and returned to his hometown. More important is what lies beneath: the inbred politics of a small agrarian community, racial attitudes towards the aboriginal community, and the mysteries of Cashin's past, which make him a laconic loner isolated from society.

In the UK *The Broken Shore* won the Crime Writers' Association's Gold Dagger Award for best novel of the year. Peter travelled to the UK in 2007 to receive his award. He thanked me in his speech for having bought his life's work for less than the price of a second-hand car. I like to think that he meant this not as a reprimand but as a gesture of affection.

Peter Temple was not an Australian by birth. He was born in South Africa in 1946 and emigrated first to Germany, then to Australia, to avoid association with racist attitudes. I believe there is an autobiographical vein in the creation of his lead character, Joe Cashin, a man whose outlook on life has been disfigured by the ugliness of racism, poverty and prejudice.

36. *The Broken Shore*

It's hard to know where to start praising this book. Plot, style, setting and characters are all startlingly good. *The Broken Shore* is one of those watershed books that makes you rethink your ideas about reading.

The Sydney Morning Herald

Peter **TEMPLE**

THE BROKEN SHORE

The
Tenderness
of Wolves

STEF PENNEY

The Tenderness of Wolves by Stef Penney was a first novel recommended to me by my former wife, Rosie de Courcy, who was working for Little, Brown at the time. They had rejected it. We took it on board. *Tenderness* became a number-one bestseller and won both the 2006 Costa Award for First Novel and the Costa Award for Book of the Year.

The first sentence remains etched in my mind: 'The last time I saw Laurent Jammet, he was in Scott's store with a dead wolf on his shoulders.' The storyline follows the quest of a distraught mother for the killer who kidnapped her daughter and murdered the fur trapper Jammet. Her quest takes her on a journey into the icy landscapes of the Canadian Arctic. The authenticity of her narrative and the epic quality of the writing are all the more remarkable because Stef Penney suffered from acute agoraphobia and had never been to Canada.

37. *The Tenderness of Wolves*

A first-rate gripper… with far greater ambitions than your average thriller, combining as it does the themes of Conrad's *Heart of Darkness*, with Atwood's *Survival*, and lashing them to a story that morphs into Ian Rankin.

The Globe and Mail

The Secret History of the World by Jonathan Black is an encyclopaedic history of man, myth and magic, lore and tradition. It is also a genuine work of scholarship, elegantly written, deeply researched and comprehensive in content. A number of the reviews described it as a masterpiece.

The author takes the reader on a unique and dizzying journey that encompasses the cults of the pharaohs, the teachings of the Buddha, the wisdom of Athena, the doctrines of Mithras, the mission of the Templars, the mysticism of Tolstoy, and the beliefs of Jung, Lenin, Philip K. Dick and Lewis Carroll. Amongst many others.

Jonathan Black is a pseudonym. Behind the mask is Mark Booth, a fellow publisher who was at the time the Publishing Director of the Century division within Random House UK. To thank me for publishing his book, and to acknowledge me as the founder of Century, Mark invited me to make a presentation to his team, an act of generosity which I have not forgotten.

38. *The Secret History of the World*

Maddening, challenging, provoking and inspiring, beautifully written. My mind is on fire with argument and wonder.

Anne Rice, author of *Interview with the Vampire*

THE SECRET
HISTORY OF
THE WORLD

JONATHAN BLACK

MEASURING
THE WORLD

DANIEL KEHLMANN
TRANSLATED BY CAROL BROWN JANEWAY

Measuring The World (2005) by Daniel Kehlmann is a novella that compares and contrasts the discoveries of two intellectual giants in the history of science. The first was Alexander von Humboldt (1769–1859), a Prussian aristocrat and indefatigable explorer who navigated the Orinoco, scaled the highest known mountain in the world clad in a tweed jacket, and returned home to record his life's journals in 400 fat volumes. Friedrich Gauss (1777–1855) was an astronomer and mathematician who travelled the world not on his feet but through a telescope and deduced by the pure application of thought and logic that space is curved.

Measuring The World is a literary gem, beautifully crafted, succinct and profound.

The most successful novel we published at Quercus was Stieg Larsson's *Girl with the Dragon Tattoo* (2005). The book had already enjoyed a phenomenal success in Sweden but it had a less than straightforward path to English-language publication.

39. *Measuring The World*

Measuring the World has proved nothing less than a literary sensation. The novel has sold more than 600,000 copies in Germany, knocking JK Rowling and Dan Brown off the bestseller lists... 31-year-old Daniel Kehlmann is a literary wunderkind already being compared to Nabokov and Proust.

The *Guardian*

Christopher MacLehose, former publisher of Harvill Press and head of Quercus's MacLehose Press imprint – a man with a distinguished track record of publishing foreign-language fiction in translation – was concerned by the poor quality of the English translation of the book when it was offered to us. I persuaded Christopher to take on the editing of the translation himself, which he did, and we duly paid an advance of £30,000 for World English translation rights.

I offered the new translation to all the usual suspects in New York and they all turned it down. Rather than approach a second echelon of lesser publishing houses, I went back to all the houses who had already rejected the book, only this time I contacted not the editors but the chief executives to whom they were responsible.

Two of the players, Sonny Mehta at Knopf and Michael Pietsch at Hachette, came up with the identical bid of $300,000. I asked both to make a final bid and undertook to accept the higher offer. Pietsch wouldn't budge. Mehta returned with a complex performance bonus scheme based on the number and position of listings on *The New York Times* bestseller charts.

Two years later, Knopf sent Quercus a cheque for $10 million. Sonny Mehta also sent me, as a personal thank-you

40. *The Girl with the Dragon Tattoo*

So much more than a thriller, *The Girl with the Dragon Tattoo* is a dazzling novel of big ideas. It tackles issues of power, corruption, justice and innocence – all the while drawing you into the twists and turns of a frighteningly suspenseful mystery.

Harlan Coben

*"A gripping crime debut
that lives up to the hype"*
JOAN SMITH, *Sunday Times*

THE GIRL WITH THE
DRAGON TATTOO

STIEG LARSSON

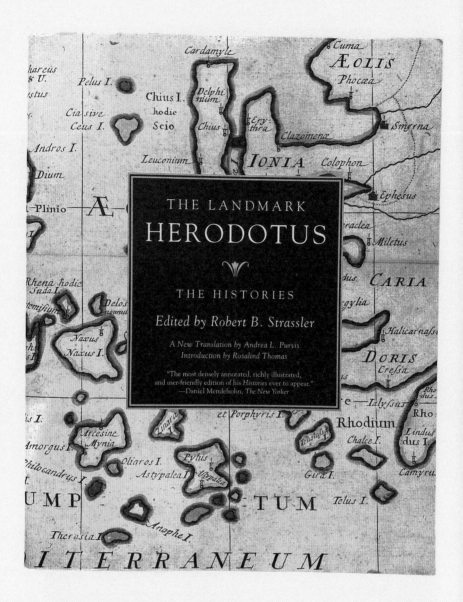

THE LANDMARK
HERODOTUS

❦

THE HISTORIES

Edited by Robert B. Strassler

A New Translation by Andrea L. Purvis
Introduction by Rosalind Thomas

"The most densely annotated, richly illustrated,
and user-friendly edition of his *Histories* ever to appear."
—Daniel Mendelsohn, *The New Yorker*

present, tickets for Wagner's *Ring* cycle at the Metropolitan Opera House.

I revere Herodotus as the father of history and admire The Landmark edition as a monument of scholarship. Herodotus gives a full account of the Persian Wars (499 BC–449 BC) in which a confederation of Greek city states defeated the empire of Cyrus the Great, and thereby saved the heritage of classical civilisation in the West from destruction by a despot in the East.

The one thousand pages of The Landmark Herodotus offer a great more than a military history of the Persian Wars. The father of history was not only a great historian but also an ace reporter, an inveterate traveller and a superb storyteller.

Quercus Giants was an awesome list of illustrated books on subjects that included the history of the cosmos, antique maps of the world, an atlas of planet Earth as seen from space, and naval vessels in the age of sail. We shall not see their like again. These books are so big that no bookcase can accommodate them and so heavy that it takes a trolley to transport them. The only printer capable

41. *The Landmark Herodotus*

Herodotus of Halicarnassus here presents his research so that human events do not fade with time. May the great and wonderful deeds – some brought forth by the Hellenes, others by the barbarians – not go unsung, as well as the causes that led them to make war upon one another.

The opening lines of Herodotus's *Histories*

of printing the Quercus Giants was based in Chengdu, in southwestern China, and they had to bus in field labourers to sew bindings strong enough to stop the books falling apart. The retail price was set at £50.00.

The Quercus team basked in the sunshine of our success. We were twice presented with a Nibbie award at the annual prize-giving sponsored by *Publishing News*. We rented a handsome eighteenth-century town house in Bloomsbury, next door to Faber & Faber (who handled our sales), and ate our lunchtime sandwiches in our own little garden under the shade of *Ailanthus altissima*, the Tree of Heaven.

But a serpent was waiting for us in the undergrowth.

ooooo

The habitually cheerful Mark Smith would succumb from time to time to blinding headaches so severe that he had to take to his bed in a darkened room, sometimes for days on end. When the migraines lifted a different personality took over. Mark told me that ever since he was knee-high to a grasshopper he had known he was bound to succeed. He was the most generous of friends. His optimism acknowledged no boundaries. He would answer any challenge, however improbable, with a phrase that became his trademark: 'Oh, OK.'

Our partnership foundered, alas, on a disagreement over the future management of the business. Mark wanted to appoint his golfing companion David North, formerly a sales manager at William Collins, to head the publishing programme. I felt that David was unqualified for the role. Mark and I agreed that we should ask a non-executive director with a financial background in the City to review the pros and cons and arbitrate between us. But he came up with a report so distorted and disingenuous that it eventually broke the bonds of my partnership with Mark.

This came as a massive disappointment. No company of which I was a part had or has achieved so much in so many categories in such a short time as Quercus. After several weeks of fruitless negotiation with Mark and Wayne, I turned in my resignation and followed my son Nic Cheetham to join him at Atlantic Books.

16

Atlantic Books
2009–11
Corvus and cash crises

The three years with Atlantic began with a bang and ended in a whimper. The boss was Toby Mundy, a formidable intellectual and a gifted publisher. He brought together an extraordinary array of international talent.

His editor-in-chief was Ravi Mirchandani, a man with an uncanny talent for picking winners in the field of literary fiction. Morgan Entrekin was the owner of Grove Atlantic, one of the leading literary boutiques in New York. Patrick Gallagher, CEO of Allen and Unwin in Australia, appointed Atlantic as their distributor in the UK. Nic and I joined the company to develop a new commercial imprint, Corvus, to stand alongside Atlantic.

Collectively, this line-up looked like a ministry of all the talents. Atlantic published Aravind Adiga from India (winner of the 2008 Booker Prize), Richard Flanagan and Christos Tsiolkas from Australia, Rian Malan and Damon Galgut from South Africa, Neil Stephenson and Joyce Carol Oates from America, and a novel, *In For a Penny In For a*

Pound (2010), from Tim Waterstone, the founder of a well-known chain of book shops in the UK.

Nonetheless, it ended in tears. I forbear to mention the name of the ironically dubbed Wizard of the West responsible for mismanaging the accounts or dwell on the eye-popping losses we incurred as a result.

On a summer weekend in 2011, Toby called me at home to ask whether I would like to volunteer for redundancy or prefer to stay on as a Non-Executive Director with a ringside seat at the endgame. It was hardly a difficult decision, as there was no more cash in the till. My short but eventful time at Atlantic was up.

17

Head of Zeus
2012–24
Pink chairs and beautiful books

The Corvus team abandoned Atlantic at the end of 2011 to set up shop in Monmouth Street in Seven Dials. We rented an attic in the office of the literary agent David Godwin, scavenged six pink plastic chairs from Heal's, named ourselves Head of Zeus – generally shortened to HoZ by insiders and intimates – and adopted the owl of Athena as our symbol of wisdom.

The first new executive to join the team was Clémence Jacquinet, who came in as a freelancer to oversee the production of our first book. Clémence has played a key role in the strategy of making beautiful books with a generous complement of illustrations, elegant design and high production values ever since.

Our first publication was Robert K. Massie's biography of Catherine the Great. Bob Massie was already a friend, well known as a world-class historian. At Orion we had inherited his first and evergreen bestseller *Nicholas and Alexandra* when we acquired Victor Gollancz in 1998. I was riveted by his masterpiece of naval history, *Castles of Steel* (published by Random House in 2003). But what drew me to *Catherine the Great* was not only the reputation of the author but also the extraordinary life story of his subject.

She was born in 1729 as Princess Sophia Augusta Frederica of Anhalt-Zerbst. Her father was the military governor of an unimportant garrison town on the Baltic. In the course of a long and extraordinary life, she travelled to St Petersburg in 1745 as the bride-to-be of the heir to the Russian throne, renounced her Catholic faith, changed her name to Catherine, consigned her husband to an asylum, bedded the greatest soldier of her day, extended the boundaries of her adopted country to the Black Sea, introduced a raft of social reforms, corresponded with the intellectual giants of the Enlightenment and won the hearts of all the Russians. She died in 1796 and remains the only female monarch known to history as 'the Great'.

42. *Catherine the Great*

Massie, who has spent almost half a century studying czarist Russia, has always been a biographer with the instincts of a novelist.

The New York Times

Catherine
THE GREAT

·

PORTRAIT OF A WOMAN

·

ROBERT K.MASSIE

PULITZER PRIZE–WINNING AUTHOR
OF *PETER THE GREAT* **AND** *NICHOLAS AND ALEXANDRA*

CIXIN LIU

TRANSLATED BY KEN LIU

THE THREE-BODY PROBLEM

At the start Head of Zeus were among the pioneers of ebook publishing, working in partnership with Amazon to sell mass-market genre fiction at bargain-basement prices. In the early years this proved to be a lucrative strategy. We won a number of awards for our digital skills and data management.

Amanda Ridout joined us as Managing Director in 2013. She had an impressive CV as an energetic divisional manager at Hodder Headline. She had also spent three years as CEO of Phaidon, one of the leading art book publishers in the UK.

Amanda moved quickly to develop and expand our position as a leader in digital publishing. She brought in Caroline Ridding, a senior supermarket book buyer from Tesco, to head a new imprint specialising in mass-market women's fiction. Caroline had a formidable reputation. Regrettably, the terms of her contract with Head of Zeus became a bone of contention between us. After a prolonged and fruitless period of negotiation, in 2017 I made both Caroline and Amanda redundant and asked them to leave the company.

43. *The Three-Body Problem*

A breakthrough book… a unique blend of scientific and philosophical speculation, politics and history, conspiracy theory and cosmology, where kings and emperors from both Western and Chinese history mingle in a dreamlike game world, while cops and physicists deal with global conspiracies, murders, and alien invasions in the real world.

Review by George R. R. Martin

My decision was opposed by a number of our senior staff, including Nic Cheetham and Rosie de Courcy. An Extraordinary Board Meeting was called and put to the vote of all our shareholders. Had I lost the vote, I would have been forced to resign. As it turned out I survived by a whisker. Amanda and Caroline left to start Boldwood Books. I remained in place as Executive Chairman of Head of Zeus. This was in all respects a deeply uncomfortable episode.

'Even What Doesn't Happen Is Epic' was the banner headline of the front-page review in the *London Review of Books* on publication of Cixin Liu's masterwork. We published the first volume, *The Three Body Problem*, and its sequel, *The Dark Forest*, in 2015, and the final volume, *Death's End*, in 2016. Everything to do with these books is off the scale: the number of pages, the sales figures, the awards and the scope of a story that takes the reader beyond the heat death of the universe to the very end of time.

In the course of the 1,500 pages of his text, the Master explores not only the laws of time and space but also the nature of humankind, the art of politics, the fatal impact of a higher civilisation on a less developed culture, and the

44. *That Glimpse of Truth*

Profound, lyrical, shocking, wise, the short story is capable of almost anything. This collection of 100 of the finest stories ever written ranges from the essential to the unexpected, the traditional to the surreal... childhood favourites and national treasures, Booker Prize winners and Nobel Laureates.

From the Editor's Introduction

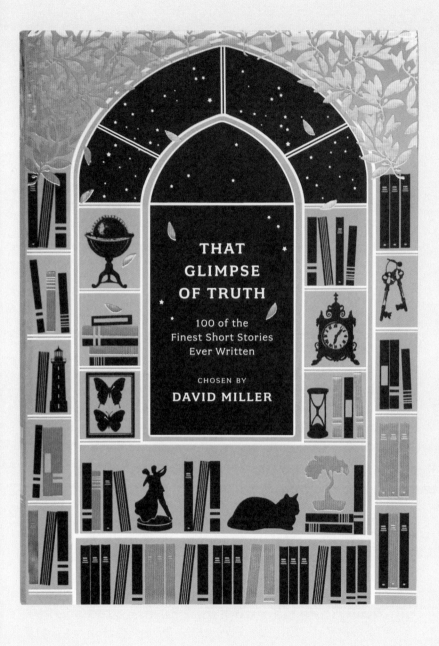

THAT GLIMPSE OF TRUTH

100 of the
Finest Short Stories
Ever Written

CHOSEN BY
DAVID MILLER

genius of individuals whose insights have the power to alter the course of history.

All of these are delivered with an inscrutable smile and a gentle touch of humour from the foremost science-fiction imagination of our time.

The Netflix adaptation of the trilogy premiered on 21 March 2024. Ahead of its release rumours abounded: the production costs of the series could match the national debt of a nation; the screenwriting duo of David Benioff and D. B. Weiss, creators of *Game of Thrones*, were to receive $200,000,000 for their services. Estimates of the production budget soared up to $1 billion.

ooooo

David Miller's *That Glimpse of Truth* (2014), an anthology of the world's best short stories, runs to 946 pages, roves over the entire time span of the written word, and acknowledges no boundaries of language or geography. It is, perhaps, the most ambitious undertaking that I have witnessed, and one of the most rewarding.

That Glimpse of Truth was a model for the anthologies we have published since. These include fiction and non-fiction, poetry and prose. They vary in extent from six hundred to a thousand pages. The subjects covered range from genre fiction to history, travel, adventure, science and philosophy. We face little competition: the sheer extent of our anthologies and the cost of clearing the permission fees act as a serious deterrent to any potential rivals.

My personal favourites include *We, Robots: Artificial Intelligence in 100 Stories* (2020), edited by Simon Ings; *The Wild Isles: An Anthology of the Best of British and Irish Nature Writing* (2021), selected by Patrick Barkham; and *Funny Ha Ha: 80 of the Funniest Stories Ever Written* (2019), selected and introduced by Paul Merton.

Silver Wheel (2016) by Elen Elenna is the work of a professional shaman. Her book celebrates a world that predates the invention of the gods. She writes about the healing powers of nature, the freedom of the spirit, the garden of Eden in the absence of original sin. The business she founded is conducted online from her home in Glastonbury, offering group seminars and individual tuition to an international following across the world.

Elen Elenna is my daughter, the most adventurous and independent of my children. Ten years earlier we travelled together in Italy and in Greece to explore the heritage of the classical world. In southern Italy we visited the Bay of Naples, the slopes of Mount Vesuvius, the island of Capri and the summer palace of Tiberius. In Rome, the Pantheon of Agricola and the treasures of the Vatican. The standard fare of the tourist traffic.

Greece was a different matter. On arrival at the Hotel Grande Bretagne in Athens, we rented a car and quartered the country from the Albanian border in the north to the Mani peninsula in the south. We had booked no hotels and took pot luck in bed and breakfast homes and hostels, ate lunch at seaside tavernas, rose with the dawn and bedded down at nightfall.

I can't claim to be entirely unbiased when I say that the landscapes of Greece in the early spring are the most beautiful on earth. Every verge, plain and mountain is alive with wildflowers and blossom. Window boxes of pink and scarlet geraniums decorate every village. Every bend in the road can open up a new panorama of distant mountains or a glimpse of the wine-dark sea on the horizon.

We consulted the Oracle at Delphi, climbed Mount Olympus on 25 March, Greece's National Day of Independence, paid tribute to the 300 Spartans who died at the hot gates of Thermopylae, gazed into the ravine of the River

Aoös in the Zagoria, which runs deeper than the Grand Canyon in America. It was here that Elen sat on the edge of the abyss with her legs dangling over the edge and declared that if there ever was a paradise, this must be it.

We turned south from Epirus to Missolonghi, where Byron died of malaria in April 1824, pressed on to Olympia in the Peloponnese, where the Olympic Games took place over a period of twelve centuries from the eighth century BC to the fourth century AD, then down to the ancient battlements of Monemvasia.

On a clear day you can look out from the battlements to the distant outline of Crete and marvel that traders plied these waters more than twenty-five centuries ago carrying goods to and from the Egypt of the Pharaohs and the Phoenicians in the Levant.

I am deeply beholden to Elen for her company on our excursion into the Classical Age of Ancient Greece. Nevertheless, there is still a mystery that needs to be resolved. How did the Greeks come up with the epics of Homer, the philosophy of Plato, the plays of Euripides, the science of Aristotle, the poetry of Sappho, the mathematics of Euclid, the histories of Herodotus, the politics of Sophocles, and spin a web of gods, demigods and heroes that cloaks their world in a gossamer of myth and magic?

45. *Silver Wheel*

A precious treasure of lost Lemurian wisdom is found in the forest. It is a book, clad in worn white deerskin, and written within on pages of bark is inscribed a mysterious and glowing script. It is written in the language of the Elven Ones, who long ago vanished from our world.

Excerpt from the author's description of her book

ELEN ELENNA

SILVER
WHEEL

The Lost Teachings of the
Deerskin Book

DAN JONES

AUTHOR OF *THE PLANTAGENETS* AND *THE TEMPLARS*

POWERS

✦—— AND ——✦

THRONES

A NEW HISTORY OF
THE MIDDLE AGES

Powers And Thrones: A New History of the Middle Ages (2021) by Dan Jones is a 700-page history of Medieval Europe with a time span from the sack of Rome in AD 410 to the early years of the Renaissance. It was Dan's third consecutive national bestseller following *The Templars* (2017) and *Crusaders* (2019) and has become the most successful history book published to date under our Apollo imprint.

Dan is a miraculous juggler, with the stamina to deliver a fistful of marvels all at the same time: limpid prose, impeccable scholarship, high-octane excitement, boundless energy and a dramatic imagination.

These qualities are not Dan's only contribution to the fortunes of our company. In 2022 he made his debut as a novelist with *Essex Dogs*, the first in a trilogy, and another national bestseller. He chairs a panel of advisers on the development of our history list. In this role he has brought us a powerhouse of outstanding writers including Emma Wells, author of *Heaven on Earth* (2022); Elodie Harper, author of *The Wolf Den* (2021); and Honor Cargill-Martin, author of *Messalina* (2023). Dan has generously dedicated *Powers and Thrones*: 'For Anthony who thinks of everything'. I can only respond by dedicating this chapter of my career: 'To Dan who actually makes everything happen'.

46. *Powers And Thrones*

Words are heavily loaded... Medieval is frequently employed as a dirty term, particularly by newspaper editors, who use it as shorthand when they want to suggest stupidity, barbarity and wanton violence.

From the author's introduction

ooooo

Richard Dawkins is two years older than I am and we were both undergraduates at Balliol at much the same time. But we didn't actually meet until the launch of *River Out of Eden* (1995), which was published in the Science Masters series in my Orion days.

The Ancestor's Tale, published by Weidenfeld & Nicolson in 2004, is the most ambitious book we have worked on together – an 800-page ride in a time machine that transports the reader backwards on a genetic journey from the present day to the origins of life. This was a big ask, even for the Professor for the Public Understanding of Science, and I had to pay an embarrassingly large advance for the privilege of publishing it.

We parted company when I declined to make an offer for his atheist manifesto *The God Delusion* (2006) – not on theological grounds, but because I didn't believe it would sell. It went on to sell several million copies.

In 2021 we regrouped to publish *Flights of Fancy*, a co-production between Richard and his partner Jana Lenzová, in which Richard explains the physics, biology and

47. *Flights of Fancy*

Dawkins is both a profoundly original scientific thinker and a marvellously adept explainer.

The New York Times

Like Steven Pinker's *How the Mind Works* or Stephen Hawking's *Brief History of Time*, it's a one-stop education, a marathon of the mind.

Newsday

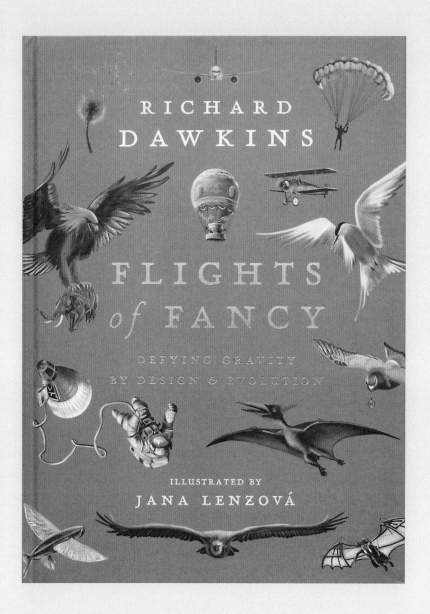

RICHARD DAWKINS

FLIGHTS *of* FANCY

DEFYING GRAVITY
BY DESIGN & EVOLUTION

ILLUSTRATED BY
JANA LENZOVÁ

evolution of flight. Jana is an artist who met Richard when she was commissioned to translate *The God Delusion* into Slovak. Her paintings and sketches illumine everything that defies the power of gravity, from seed pods to aeroplanes. My special favourite, perhaps because we share a Mexican origin, is the pterosaur *Quetzalcoatlus*, the largest bird that ever flew.

Flights of Fancy was originally intended for young adults, but the marriage of text and illustrations seduces readers of all ages and habitats. We have sold foreign co-editions across the globe in twenty languages.

Richard continues to produce extraordinary books. In the autumn of 2024 Head of Zeus published his 'Darwinian Reverie', *The Genetic Book of the Dead*, described by Steven Pinker as 'overflowing with the beauty of nature, the beauty of language, and the beauty of ideas'.

18

Bloomsbury

2021–4

A proposition at the Palace

In the autumn of 2018, Queen Camilla, then Duchess of Cornwall, hosted a party at Buckingham Palace to celebrate the fiftieth anniversary of the Booker Prize. Foremost among the eminent publishers and the literary lions present was Bloomsbury's Nigel Newton. Bloomsbury was the publisher of Michael Ondaatje's *The English Patient*, joint winner of the prize in 1992, and now recipient of the Golden Man Booker Award for the best of the best.

Prompted by several glasses of champagne, my wife Georgina suggested to Nigel that Bloomsbury should buy Head of Zeus and add it to its empire. He and I had been friends for decades, ever since the days when I was in charge of Century Hutchinson and he was the home sales manager at Sidgwick & Jackson. Nigel and I used to meet annually at the Frankfurt Book Fair in Jimmy's Bar, a basement haunt for late-night drinkers, to exchange war stories and place wagers payable in vintage wines.

Nigel agreed that he and I would explore the idea of selling HoZ to Bloomsbury. Georgina took a snapshot of Nigel and myself grinning inanely at the camera in the forecourt of the Palace. It took a while to come to fruition, with spirited – although good natured – negotiations, but eventually a deal was agreed by Bloomsbury's Board of Directors, and the sale was announced on 2 June 2021.

∞∞∞

Liu Cixin's *The Three-Body Problem* trilogy stands at the apex of Ad Astra, Head of Zeus's Science Fiction and Fantasy list. But the sheer range and quality of the list is hard to convey without reference to a number of other authors whom we have assembled over the past decade. Collectively they represent a galaxy of talent in contemporary science fiction.

Firefall (2014) by Peter Watts is an omnibus edition of two earlier stories – *Blindsight* (2006) and *Echopraxia* (2014). His theme is the first contact with an extraterrestrial visitor, a machine entity with unknown motives and terrifying powers. The story opens in 1982 when 62,000 mysterious objects plunge into Earth's atmosphere and execute a 360-degree survey of our home planet. It ranges into a far future where genetically modified humans venture into space to investigate the invaders. It delivers persuasive theories on the meaning of consciousness and the nature of artificial intelligence. The journey is sometimes playful, sometimes gruesome but never boring.

Adrian Tchaikovsky's *Dogs of War* (2017), *Bear Head* (2021) and *City of Last Chances* (2022) mark him out as one of the best British science-fiction writers of our time.

America's A. G. Riddle has entered the bestseller lists in the US and the UK with his cosmic adventures *Lost in Time* (2022) and *Quantum Radio* (2023).

Ken Liu is the Chinese-American author of The Dandelion Dynasty (2015–2022), a fantasy series that has given birth to a genre known as Silk Punk: gossamer balloons command the skies above and intelligent whales patrol the oceans beneath.

Lavie Tidhar is an Israeli polymath. In his two fantasy novels, *By Force Alone* (2020) and *The Hood* (2021), he distils the folklore of Britannia into a spicy brew of gangsters and warlords, magi and mystics.

In 2022 we published Lavie's 600-page magnum opus *Maror*, a fictional history of the State of Israel. The reviews were stupendous. The *Guardian* called it a masterpiece of the sacred and the profane. Other critics described it as the Jewish *Godfather* and made comparisons to Balzac and Dickens. But my favourite quote came from Junot Díaz: 'Some write in ink, others in song, Tidhar writes in fire.'

ooooo

The Known Unknowns by Lawrence M. Krauss offers his readers an eye-opening trip to the far frontiers of knowledge. Scientific discovery tends to move forward in two distinctive phases, first the formulation of theory, then the hunt for proof that will validate the theory. The theorists are usually the ones who grab the headlines. This book is an encyclopaedia, not of theory, but of what we know that we don't know, delivered in thirty-three pithy essays and addressed to a non-specialist readership.

LMK has an impressive CV as a professor of theoretical physics, as an eminent public intellectual and as an author. But in 2018 he was asked to resign his professorship at Arizona State University in the wake of allegations of sexual misconduct, following which he succumbed to a period of depression.

It was at this point that Richard Dawkins introduced him to Head of Zeus. We published his next book, *The Physics of Climate Change*, in 2020, and prodded him gently into writing *The Known Unknowns*.

We sent an early proof copy of *The Known Unknowns* to Stephen Fry, whose online podcast has several million followers. He describes it as 'A book that reawakens wonder'. Our edition now carries endorsements from Martin Rees, Noam Chomsky and Anthony Grayling, as well as Richard Dawkins.

Frederick the Second by Ernst Kantorowicz (1895–1963) tells the story of the last Hohenstaufen Holy Roman Emperor (1225–50), polyglot ruler of a vast swathe of western Europe from Germany to Sicily and an energetic patron of the arts and sciences. He is known to history as *stupor mundi*, the 'wonder of the world'.

Not only is Kantorowicz's book a monument of medieval scholarship, it is also one of the finest works of literature in the German language. I first read *Frederick the Second* when I was an undergraduate at Balliol, but it was not until 2019 that Head of Zeus published a new edition with an introduction written by Dan Jones.

48. *The Known Unknowns*

What an achievement: science, the beauty of science, the adventure of science so well expressed. Even a wretched innumerate like me can grasp the excitement of the key stories in discovery that Lawrence Krauss tells with such splendid clarity.

Stephen Fry

'Lawrence Krauss is one of our finest and most readable celebrators and explicators of science, and in *The Known Unknowns* he has found his perfect subject.' **IAN McEWAN**

THE KNOWN UNKNOWNS

THE UNSOLVED MYSTERIES OF THE COSMOS

LAWRENCE M. KRAUSS

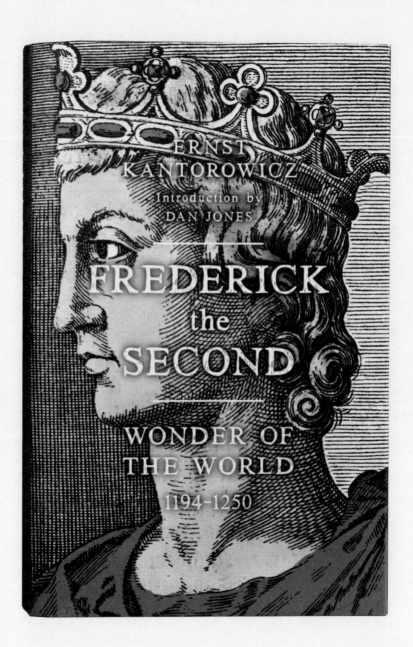

ERNST
KANTOROWICZ

Introduction by
DAN JONES

FREDERICK
the
SECOND

WONDER OF
THE WORLD

1194–1250

When J. W. von Goethe visited Sicily in 1787, he declared that the island's history was the clue to everything. For three thousand years it was the fulcrum between the continents of Asia, Africa and Europe. Its fertile plains and forested mountains were prized and contested by Phoenicians, Greeks, Romans, Arabs and Normans.

In 1198 both the Norman kingdom of Sicily and the Hohenstaufen kingdom of Germany were inherited by the three-year-old Frederick in Palermo. He was dubbed 'the boy from Apulia'. For much of his youth he ran riot in the streets of the capital, learned the languages of his subjects – Arabic, French, Sicilian and German – and was schooled in the arts of statecraft.

For the greater part of his reign Frederick was called upon to defend and preserve his dual heritage north and south of the Alps. He was challenged on his home ground by the Papacy, which, under the leadership of Innocent III, laid claim to the authority of the Holy Roman Emperors; in Germany by the rebel Dukes of Swabia; and in the Crusader Kingdoms of the Holy Land by the military

49. *Frederick the Second*

On Sunday 18 March 1229 Frederick II Hohenstaufen, Holy
Roman Emperor, tyrant of Sicily, ruler of Italians and
Germans and bane of the popes, marched into the Church
of the Holy Sepulchre, snatched the crown of Jerusalem from
the high altar and placed it on his own head.

From Dan Jones's introduction to the Head of Zeus edition (2019)

genius of Saladin, who reclaimed Jerusalem in the name of the Prophet.

It was not until the last fifteen years of his reign that Frederick was able to indulge his real interests and demonstrate the full range of his talents. He left a trail of castles and hunting lodges across his domains; he travelled with a zoo of exotic animals in his train, and an elite of Muslim crossbowmen as his bodyguards. He corresponded in six different languages with scientists, philosophers and men of letters, and founded a university in Naples. He wrote a treatise on falconry, *De arte venandi cum avibus* (On the Art of Hunting with Birds), which remained the standard textbook for the next 400 years.

Fate had one last irony in store for the Wonder of the World: he was the last of his line, the last Hohenstaufen Holy Roman Emperor, the last Hohenstaufen King of Germany and the last King of Jerusalem. *Sic transit stupor mundi*. He died at the age of fifty-five on 13 December 1250. His sarcophagus is to be found in Palermo Cathedral.

ooooo

Before moving on to the last of my fifty books, I owe a vote of thanks to Neil Belton, the Editorial Director who acquired it. I have known Neil for thirty years and more, since our paths first crossed at Century Hutchinson.

50. *The Question to which the Universe is the Answer*

Pulitzer Prize-winning science journalist Natalie Wolchover's remarkable book, in which she weaves together the ideas and controversies of fundamental physics into a coherent narrative, will be published by Head of Zeus in 2026.

He is one of the most gifted publishers I have worked with. He can be grumpy and difficult, but appears to know everything about everything, from particle physics to world literature. He has twice taken home the Nibbie for best editor from publishing's annual award ceremony. He is himself an author. In 2003 I commissioned from him a novel, *A Game with Sharpened Knives* (2005), about Erwin Schrödinger, one of the pioneers in quantum mechanics, who taught us that particles could exist in two places at the same time.

I had spent years trying to press-gang Neil into accepting a job at one of my companies. It was not until he fell out with Faber & Faber in 2014 that I was able to welcome him aboard at HoZ.

Neil is an Irishman who exiled himself to England after a Marxist revolutionary phase at University College Dublin. He has given us a string of Irish bestsellers, most notably Fintan O'Toole's masterpiece on the history of modern Ireland. *We Don't Know Ourselves* (2021) was not only the bestselling book of the year in Ireland but also listed as a national bestseller by *The New York Times* in the USA and by the *Sunday Times* in the UK.

Natalie Wolchover, the author of *The Question to which the Universe is the Answer*, is an outstandingly successful British-born science journalist. In 2013, at the age of twenty-seven, she was one of the founders of *Quanta Magazine*. Her articles have also been published in *Nature*, *The New Yorker* and *The Atlantic*. She was awarded the Pulitzer Prize for Explanatory Reporting in 2022. Her special interests include particle physics, quantum computing, gravitational waves and astrophysics.

The question she addresses in her first book is this: how do we come to live in a universe where the laws of physics appear to be quite so bizarre, improbable and hard to explain? And her answer is: because our universe could not otherwise have come into existence.

My knowledge of quantum physics is not equal to the task of understanding either the question or the answer. I stand here, bemused and amazed, a short-lived hominid stranded on an insignificant planet circling a sun with a limited lifespan in a universe that winked into existence, for reasons unknown, 13.5 billion years ago.

19

The Future of Book Publishing

Times change and
we change with them

O ur most immediate problem is the yawning gap
between supply and demand. We publish too many
books, over 100,000 titles per annum. Booksellers simply
don't have the shelf space to accommodate them.

Publishers are well aware of the gap between supply
and demand, which has led to a reduction in unit sales.
In many cases the major conglomerates have sought to
compensate for the loss of income by trimming production
costs, forcing senior staff into retirement at the age of sixty,
and conducting their business online to reduce the expense
of rented office space.

An equally dubious stratagem is to look for growth by
encouraging internal competition between their own imprints. Why confine yourself to a single imprint in any given
genre if you can have two or more? It actually increases the
oversupply of titles on the market, promotes office politics,
and creates a new layer of bureaucracy to police the rules on
who can offer how much to whom.

A problem which will afflict all publishers in the future is the growing competition for rights income between agents and publishers. Rights income makes a very important contribution to a publisher's profit and loss account. This becomes all the more important as the unit sales of physical books decline.

Agencies such as Curtis Brown and United Agents have already adopted a business model in which they can offer their authors a comprehensive service covering the entire spectrum of intellectual property rights, from US and translation rights to film, video, television, theatre and merchandising.

There is, regrettably, one more facet of the decline in our industry that no one wants to talk about but everyone has to accept. Books are losing their readers to the streaming platforms. The streamers are investing billions in new series because that's where the money is made. The joy of bingeing.

Nonetheless, traditional publishers who love books for what they are will not disappear. We can reinvent ourselves as luxury boutiques catering to a limited but well-heeled readership of fellow bibliophiles. In short, by returning to the vision and values of the Renaissance printers, patrons and collectors of the age of Gutenberg.

ooooo

ADDENDUM

While writing this memoir I have come to realise how difficult it is to focus on just fifty of the most memorable books that have crossed my path. The five champions listed below are the ones I am most reluctant to exclude.

Inside The Third Reich ALBERT SPEER

Not only the most significant personal German account to come out of the war but the most revealing document on the Hitler phenomenon yet written... The Führer emerges as neither an incompetent nor a carpet-gnawing madman, but as an evil genius endowed with an ineffable personal magic.

The New York Times

Albert Speer, an architect by profession, was appointed Hitler's armaments minister in 1942 and played a key role in keeping the Nazi Wehrmacht supplied with the sinews of war.

He wrote this 800-page account of his life and his relationship with Hitler while serving a twenty-year sentence in Spandau Prison. Speer used his memoirs to distance himself from the atrocities of the Third Reich. He was, in fact, fully complicit, having joined the party in 1931 and sanctioned a brutal code of punishment for the 140,000 prisoners in his workforce. He served his sentence in full and died in 1981.

The Burgundians   BART VAN LOO

A sumptuous feast of a book. Bart Van Loo uncovers a lost
empire of mad dukes, strange delicacies and great wealth.

The Times, Books of the Year 2021

Subtitled *A Vanished Empire: A History of 1111 Years and One
Day*, this is a history of the turbulent, fabulously wealthy
medieval state between France and Germany, the cradle
of what is now the Low Countries – Belgium and the
Netherlands.

The Awakening   CHARLES FREEMAN

Charles Freeman has… amassed a vast body of knowledge on a
major subject and infused it with historical understanding and
humane wit. Above all else, he makes us realise why the twelve
centuries between late Antiquity and early Modernity remain
urgently relevant to the world of the twenty-first century.'

Paul Cartledge, Emeritus A. G. Leventis Professor of Greek Culture,
University of Cambridge

Charles Freeman's *The Awakening* is a monumental work of
scholarship in which the author illumines the cultural and
intellectual history of Medieval Europe. He takes the reader
on an exhilarating journey from the end of the Roman
Empire to the scientific revolution ushered in by Copernicus
and Isaac Newton. He shows us that history is not simply
determined by emperors and kings, battles and sieges, but by
deeper currents of thought, inquiry and discovery. He gives
us unique and detailed portraits of the medieval thinkers,
scholars and pioneers who reawakened the European mind
between 522, when the polymathic philosopher Boethius,
under sentence of death in a jailhouse, penned his beliefs in
The Consolations of Philosophy, and the year 1687, which saw

the publication of Isaac Newton's *Principia Mathematica*.
These dry words of mine altogether fail to convey the depth
of the scholarship or the colour and excitement of the stories
he has to tell. Each of his thirty-two chapters is worth a book
of its own. *The Awakening* runs to more than 800 pages and
its pages glow with colour illustrations of manuscripts and
monuments. A masterwork.

The Sons of Darkness   GOURAV MOHANTY

Like *Game of Thrones* in an Indian alternative universe...
exhilarating... heralds the arrival of a special new talent.

Dan Jones

Gourav is a young Indian writer of extravagant energy and
talent. He describes himself as a lawyer by day, a stand-
up comedian in the evening and a writer by night. He has
delivered the first in a series of fantasies inspired by the
Mahabharata of Ancient India and George R. R. Martin's
A Game of Thrones.

Enceladus   CAROLYN PORCO

Enceladus is a small, obscure moon in the orbit of Jupiter.
As a highly distinguished Professor of Astrophysics, Carolyn
Porco would not claim that she is on the verge of finding the
first proof of extraterrestrial life in our universe. Nonetheless,
as the founder and head of the Cassini Project, she may, in
the coming months, be able to announce a discovery that
ranks with those of Copernicus and Newton. She watches,
we wait.

EPILOGUE

Past, present and future

When at home, I sit in a library surrounded by the thousands of books I have inherited, published or collected during my fifty years in publishing. The library is shelved in a converted chicken barn under roof beams installed in 1831. It is designed to resemble a college library or reading room from my university days.

I recognise the dominant themes in the books assembled here. History is a looking glass to make sense of the past. The Sciences define our understanding of the cosmos and formulate projections of the future. Fiction is the playlist of what it means to be human. Philosophy is the spirit of wisdom that binds them all.

These memoirs are dedicated to all those who have helped, guided and advised me on the journey of a lifetime, and to all the authors who have entrusted their work to my care.

Bibliography

1. Homer, *The Odyssey*, trans. Emily Wilson (London: W. W. Norton & Company, 2018).

2. Crane, Walter, *The Frog Prince and Other Stories* (London: George Routledge and Sons, 1874).

3. Tolkien, J.R.R., *The Lord of the Rings* (London: Allen & Unwin, 1954).

4. Cheetham, Anthony, and Parfit, Derek (eds), *Eton Microcosm* (London: Sidgwick & Jackson, 1964).

5. Liutprand of Cremona, and Norwich, John Julius (ed.), *An Embassy to Constantinople* (London: Phoenix, 1993).

6. Mann, Thomas, *The Magic Mountain*, trans. H.T. Lowe-Porter (London: Martin Secker, 1927).

7. Herbert, Frank, *Dune* (London: Victor Gollancz, 1965).

8. Lea, Timothy, *Confessions of a Window Cleaner* (London: Sphere, 1971).

9. Marcuse, Herbert, *One-Dimensional Man* (London: Sphere, 1969).

10. Cheetham, Anthony, *The Life and Times of Richard III* (London: Weidenfeld & Nicolson, 1972).

11. Lane Fox, Robin, *Alexander the Great* (London: Penguin, 1973).

12. Wambaugh, Joseph, *The Choirboys* (London: Weidenfeld & Nicolson, 1976).

13. Follett, Ken, *Storm Island* (London: Futura Publications, 1978).

14. McCullough, Colleen, *The Thorn Birds* (London: Futura Publications, 1977).

15. Dean Foster, Alan, *Alien* (London: MacDonald General Books, 1979).

16. Sagan, Carl, *Cosmos* (London: Abacus, 1980).

17. Thompson, Flora, *The Illustrated Lark Rise to Candleford* (London: Century Publishing Co. 1983).

18. Tschiffely, A.F., *Southern Cross to Pole Star* (London: Century Hutchinson, 1982).

19. Amis, Kingsley, *The Old Devils* (London: Hutchinson, 1986).

20. Trump, Donald, *The Art of the Deal* (London: Century Hutchinson, 1988).

21. Gromyko, Andrei, *Memories* (London: Hutchinson, 1989).

22. Tolstoy, Leo, *War and Peace* (London: Walter Scott, 1889).

23. Dahl, Roald, *The Vicar of Nibbleswicke* (London: Puffin, 1991).

24. Mysterious Press (founded in 1975).

25. Okri, Ben, *The Famished Road* (London: Jonathan Cape, 1991).

26. Rankin, Ian, *Strip Jack* (London: Orion Books, 1992).

27. Connelly, Michael, *Poet* (London: Orion Books, 1996).

28. Seth, Vikram, *A Suitable Boy* (London: Orion Books, 1993).

29. Fraser, Antonia, *The Six Wives of Henry VIII* (London: Weidenfeld & Nicolson, 1972).

30. Pakenham, Thomas, *Meetings with Remarkable Trees* (London: Weidenfeld & Nicolson,1996).

31. Johnson, Paul, *The Birth of The Modern* (London: Weidenfeld & Nicolson, 1991).

32. Gaarder, Jostein, *Sophie's World* (London: Orion Children's Books, 1995).

33. Greenfield, Susan, *The Human Brain* (London: Weidenfeld & Nicolson, 1997).

34. Paver, Michelle, *Wolf Brother* (London: Orion Children's Books, 2004).

35. Harrison, M. John, *Light* (London: Victor Gollancz, 2002).

36. Temple, Peter, *The Broken Shore* (London: Quercus Books, 2006).

37. Penney, Stef, *The Tenderness of Wolves* (London: Quercus Books, 2006).

38. Black, Jonathan, *The Secret History of the World* (London: Quercus Books, 2007).

39. Kehlmann, Daniel, *Measuring the World*, trans. Carol Brown Janeway (London: Quercus Books, 2006).

40. Larsson, Stieg, *The Girl with the Dragon Tattoo* (London: Quercus Books, 2008).

41. (ed.) Strassler, Robert B., *The Landmark Herodotus* (London: Quercus Books, 2008).

42. Massie, Robert K., *Catherine the Great* (London: Head of Zeus, 2011).

43. Liu, Cixin, *The Three-Body Problem*, trans. Ken Liu, (London: Head of Zeus, 2015).

44. (ed.) Miller, David, *That Glimpse of Truth* (London: Head of Zeus, 2014).

45. Elenna, Elen, *Silver Wheel* (London: Head of Zeus, 2016).

46. Jones, Dan, *Powers and Thrones* (London: Head of Zeus, 2021).

47. Dawkins, Richard, *Flights of Fancy* (London: Head of Zeus, 2021).

48. Krauss, Lawrence M., *The Known Unknowns* (London: Head of Zeus, 2023).

49. Kantorowicz, Ernst, *Frederick the Second* (London: Head of Zeus, 2019).

50. Wolchover, Natalie, *The Question to which the Universe is the Answer* (London: Head of Zeus, 2026).

Image credits

p. 11   The author in his first car.
Author's photo

p. 12   The author and his mother.
Author's photo

p. 20   The author and his brother at Summer Fields School.
Author's photo

p. 24   The author (far right) with Jonathan Aitken (left) at Eton.
Author's photo

p. 30   The vaulted dining hall at Balliol College, Oxford.
David Iliff / Wikimedia Commons

p. 33   The title page of an edition of the collected works of Liutprand of Cremona, 1640.
Art World / Alamy Stock Photo

p. 36   *Garden in Kragerø* by Edvard Munch, 1909.
ARTGEN / Alamy Stock Photo

p. 42   The author in Norway, mid-1960s.
Author's photo

p. 55   Antonia Fraser (centre), her then-husband Hugh Fraser (left) and Jonathan Aitken (right), March 1970.
Photo by Evening Standard/Hulton Archive/ Getty Images

p. 69   Signing the contract: the author and Colleen McCullough.
Author's photo

p. 72   Robert Maxwell, 1973.
Photo by Evening Standard/Hulton Archive/ Getty Images

p. 78   L'Escargot restaurant.
Courtesy of L'Escargot

p. 86   Kingsley Amis, 1975.
Tim Graham / Getty Images

p. 102   Anthony, 1991.
Photo by Susan Wakefield

p. 108   The Mysterious Press Bookshop.
Courtesy of Otto Penzler

p. 112   Ben Okri, Oxford 2022.
Photo by David Levenson/Getty Images

p. 114   *Bookseller* cover 29 May 1992.
Author's photo

p. 137   The author interviewed in the *Independent* by Hunter Davies, 24 March 1992.
Author's photo

p. 138   *Bookseller*, 10 October 2003.
Author's photo

p. 146   The author with Mark Smith, CEO of Quercus.
Author's photo

p. 164   A Greek amphora depicting the birth of Athena, *c.* 560–540 BC.
YA/BOT / Alamy Stock Photo

p. 182   Bedford Square garden, outside the Bloomsbury offices.
Greg Balfour Evans / Alamy Stock Photo

p. 191   The evolving universe as captured by NASA's Hubble space telescope.
NASA, ESA, H. Teplitz and M. Rafelski (IPAC/ Caltech), A. Koekemoer (STScI), R. Windhorst (Arizona State University), and Z. Levay (STScI)

p. 194   Johann Gutenberg (*c.* 1400–68), inventor of the moveable type printing press. Photogravure, after a painting, 1894, by Jean Leon Gerome Ferris.
VTR / Alamy Stock Photo